Wine and Food-101

A Comprehensive Guide to Wine and the Art of Matching Wine With Food

by

John R. Fischer

authorHOUSE

1663 LIBERTY DRIVE, SUITE 200
BLOOMINGTON, INDIANA 47403
(800) 839-8640

500 AVEBURY BLVD.
CENTRAL MILTON KEYNES
UNITED KINGDOM

AuthorHouse™
1663 Liberty Drive, Suite 200
Bloomington, IN 47403
www.authorhouse.com
Phone: 1-800-839-8640

AuthorHouse™ UK Ltd.
500 Avebury Boulevard
Central Milton Keynes, MK9 2BE
www.authorhouse.co.uk
Phone: 08001974150

This book is a work of non-fiction. Unless otherwise noted, the author
and the publisher make no explicit guarantees as to the accuracy of
the information contained in this book and in some cases, names of
people and places have been altered to protect their privacy.

First published by AuthorHouse 10/19/2006

ISBN: 1-4259-1470-5 (e)
ISBN: 1-4208-8301-1 (sc)
ISBN: 1-4259-6806-6 (dj)

Library of Congress Control Number: 2005908158

Printed in the United States of America
Bloomington, Indiana

This book is printed on acid-free paper.

I would like to express my gratitude to all of those who have guided me in the construction of this book or helped in the tedious job of editing. A special thanks to Jean Devoy, Carol Fischer, Duke Matz, Steve Hipple, Harvey Hayes, Morris Caudle, Roger Peterson, Les Zanotti, Jose R. Garrigo, Mike Scott, and Jim Trebbien.

To my four grandchildren:

Michael, Madeline, Ella, and Jackson John

And grandchildren-to-be

Baby Fischer, Baby Bereson, and Baby Boy Chandler

With love and affection—

Pop

Contents

PREFACE

Time and time again, I hear the erroneous statement "It doesn't make any difference what wine you match with food. Drink the wine that you like." Once you understand the basics of matching wine with food, you will appreciate the sophistry of such statements.

Would you put mustard on ice cream or maple syrup on raw oysters? Would you wear argyle socks with an evening gown or wear a Kansas State sweatshirt to a Nebraska football game? Of course you wouldn't. Disparate combinations such as these affront our senses. They have a disjointed feel that attacks our sense of artistry. In contrast, items that match and complement each other are pleasing to our senses. Doesn't it seem logical that certain foods will have an affinity to specific wine styles?

If the pleasure of wine equals one unit, and the pleasure of food equals one unit, the idea is to make the union of wine with food equal to a pleasure of 3 or 4 or more units. In a successful wine-food pairing, the whole should always be greater than the sum of its parts: the wine enhances the food and the food heightens the character of the wine. Unfortunately, in many cases, the whole is less than the sum of its parts, as some wine-food combinations jangle the senses and create discord.

A great deal of the literature written on the subject of matching wine with food is difficult to read, difficult to understand, and even more difficult to use. Many books are filled with complicated schemes and endless lists of wine-food pairings. The opinions of one author frequently contradict those of another. One author will recommend a wine for a particular dish while another will recommend a completely different style of wine. The result is total confusion for the reader.

Too many books jump directly to the topic of matching wine with food without first developing an understanding about wine. That is like trying to read before you learn the alphabet. Knowledge about wine is the foundation from which we develop the art of marrying wine to food. Most of us have a pretty good knowledge about food— we have been eating since the day we were born. However, wine is a newer experience, and a little more complicated.

The purpose of this book is twofold: to supply the reader with a basic knowledge about wine, and to develop the expertise necessary to successfully match a wine to food. It is a book of concepts, not a long list of wine-food pairings developed through the chimerical cerebrations of some stuffy and opinionated epicurean.

Granted, there are classical wine food combinations where the wine fits the food to perfection. However, other than in ethnic restaurants, the majority of chefs do not make classical dishes. They create their own recipes from food items that are fresh and readily available. The basis of art is creativity, not copybook. Obviously, a chef must know the basics, and classical cooking is the groundwork on which skills are acquired. It is the take-off point to the creation of original dishes.

Most of the dishes found in restaurants cannot be found in some fanciful list of wine-food pairings. The only way that you can match wine to newly created recipes is by thoroughly understanding the simple concepts of matching wine with food.

This is a self-help book that will organize your approach to wine-food pairings. The concepts are simple and logical. Your newly acquired knowledge will give you much pleasure; moreover, your perspective about the culinary arts will expand from a purely mechanical level to one that is sensual, creative, and artistic.

High quality wines are works of art. The winemaker selects premium grapes and skillfully molds them into a savory beverage endowed with the artistic qualities of style, creativity, precision, balance, and finesse. However, you must have a basic knowledge about the structural makeup and the evolution of a wine to fully appreciate its artistic qualities. Once you understand wine, the artistry, sophistication, and complexities of its makeup will become evident. You will find wine to be a beverage that is both intellectually stimulating and hedonistically satisfying.

Being able to fully appreciate an art form is the essence of its enjoyment. Tasting a wine without the knowledge of what you are looking for negates a great part of the tasting experience. It's like trying to visualize a sculpture while wearing a blindfold. You can feel its contours, but the visual part—the most important part—is missing.

Food, properly prepared and skillfully presented, is one of the quintessential, but least recognized art forms. A skillful chef paints his plate with an array of colorful and tantalizing flavors that stimulate the senses and engender a feeling of pleasure unlike any other work of art. High quality wines and epicurean styled foods are evaluated by our senses, ingested, and assimilated into our very being—talk about taking-in and devouring an art form!

Connoisseurs are people who have the expertise to judge the merits of a piece of art. They use as many of their senses as possible to evaluate its worth, and then luxuriate in the pleasure that the work evokes. The connoisseur involves himself in every aspect that the work has to offer in order to appreciate the full merit of the artisan's skill.

Wines and foods are enjoyed by the senses of sight, smell, taste, and feel. It is one of the few art forms that can be appreciated by so many of our senses. This book will teach you how to utilize your senses to fully appreciate the virtues or faults of wines and food. The pleasure you derive in pairing wine with food will be greatly enhanced by your newly acquired knowledge of the culinary arts. You will have become a connoisseur.

Part 1

Wine

"Any fool can know. The point is to understand."
—Albert Einstein

CHAPTER 1
Wine Basics

WHAT IS WINE?

The dictionary defines wine as the product of fermented grape juice. However, this definition is not completely accurate as wine can also be made from the juice of other fruits such as elderberries, blackberries, or chokecherries. In this book, we will concern ourselves strictly with wine made from premium grapes. Serious wine drinkers will argue that the dictionary definition is a gross understatement, contending that there is something very special and intriguing about quality wine that is alluring, artistic, intellectually stimulating, and sensually satisfying.

The different types of grapes, such as Cabernet Sauvignon, Pinot Noir, or Chardonnay, are known as **grape varietals**. There is a plethora of different grape varietals, and each of these is capable of producing wine. However, quality wines are made from only a select group of noble varietals that are endowed with great wine making ability. The majority of grape varietals make only common wines, and even the most talented winemaker cannot make good wine out of undistinguished grapes. Lesser varietals, such as Thompson Seedless, are used to produce raisins or table grapes. They can make wine, but the final product is invariably of very inferior quality.

There are many variables that go into the production of a quality wine; however, the single most important element is the grape. The famous wine making grapes, such as Cabernet Sauvignon, Pinot Noir, and Chardonnay, have the right stuff within the berry to produce wines of exemplary quality. These grapes must be planted in specific soil under ideal climatic conditions. Grape farmers then vigilantly cultivate and carefully pick the grapes at optimal ripeness. The grapes are then crushed and placed into large vats where the grape juice, known as **must**, is converted into wine. The process in which grape juice is converted into wine is called **fermentation**. During fermentation, yeast converts grape sugars into alcohol. The winemaker either uses the natural yeast found on the grape skins, or he selects special yeast strains. Each strain of yeast will produce its own distinctive wine. It is the skill of the winemaker—with a great deal of help from Mother Nature— that changes grape juice into high quality wine. In the wine growing districts, the winemaker is a celebrity who is held in high regard because of his artistic talents.

Wine spans a spectrum from ordinary spirit lifting table wine to the magnificently complex and artistic creations sought out by wine connoisseurs worldwide. Although the majority of ultra-premium wines have shocking price tags, there are large numbers of high quality wines being produced both in this country and abroad that are very affordable. Australia, Chile, New Zealand, South Africa, and several other newcomers produce excellent wines at very affordable prices.

There is a glossary in the appendix of this book that is titled "A Wine Tasters Vocabulary." Any terms that you may not be familiar with will likely be found in this section. A working knowledge of this vocabulary will give you the language to better express the character, merits or faults of a wine.

TYPES OF WINES

There are six major types of wine: red, white, rosé (including blush wines), sparkling wines, fortified wines, and dessert wines. Most people are surprised to learn that all grape juice is white. The pigment component of red wines comes from the skins of grapes. Red wine grapes are pressed and the white juice is allowed to remain in contact with the skins. The grape juice subsequently extracts the pigment from the skins to give wine its beautiful red-purple color.

In **blush wines**, the white juice is allowed to remain in contact with the red grape skins for only a short period of time so only a small amount of pigment is extracted. White Zinfandel and similar blushes are produced in this fashion. The famous rosé wines from the Loire valley (France) are made in a similar fashion from the Grenache grape. True Rosé wines are not a blend between red and white wine varietals; indeed, such mixtures are prohibited in many locals.

In some instances, a white wine is produced from red or black colored grapes. In the process, the white juice is quickly removed from the red skins. Champagnes called *Blanc de Noirs*, are made from red grapes in this fashion.

Nevertheless, **white wines** are almost always made from white grapes. These grapes, when fully ripe are in fact green-yellow tinged in color. The yellow and green pigments in the skins give white wine its characteristic color. Chablis is often green tinted, and Gewurztraminer can have a deep golden color. German Rieslings are sweet and often almost completely colorless because their skins have a low concentration of pigment. White wines are usually lighter and tarter than the red varietals and invariably have a significantly shorter life span. Chardonnay, Sauvignon Blanc, white Bordeaux and Riesling wines are typical examples of white wines.

A **fortified wine** is one whose alcohol content is increased by the addition of alcohol. The alcoholic content in unfortified wines range from 7%—16%. Alcohol levels greater than 16% kill the yeast that ferments the wine. The alcohol content in fortified wines is increased beyond 16% by the addition of grape brandy or other spirits after fermentation is completed. Port is fortified with grape brandy to a range of 19%—21%, Sherry to 16%—20% and Madeira to18%— 20%. Sherry and Madeira can be dry or sweet; Port is invariably sweet.

In quality **dessert wines**, nearly all of the sweetness in the wine is derived from residual amounts of grape sugars, or by the addition sweet unfermented grape juice (called *süss reserve* in Germany).

THE FLAVORS IN WINE

Many people mistakenly believe that the flavors in quality wine are infused into it from external sources. With the exception of oaky flavors derived from the oak barrel in which the wine was aged or fermented, flavors in wine come strictly from the grape berry. In fact, it is against the law to infuse flavors from external sources. It is intriguing that multiple flavors such as raspberries, strawberries, mushrooms, truffles, licorice, sandalwood, spices, herbs, and the like are derived from chemical compounds within the grape berry itself. Wines with such an array of complex flavors exhibit one of the hallmarks of high quality wines: complexity. The greater the complexity, the better the wine.

As wine ages, its youthful fruity flavors, known as **aroma**, are gradually replaced by more exotic flavors such as mushrooms, truffles, smoky tobacco, leather, and spice. These largely non-fruity flavors are known as **bouquet**. The creation of bouquet occurs through chemical reactions occurring within the bottled wine as it ages.

Wine is a living beverage: it is born, matures, and dies. High quality wines can have a life span of 100 years or more. The rambunctious and aggressive nature of a young wine turns into a sophisticated beverage at maturity, and then slowly fades away and dies. During this process, the flavor profile of the wine also changes. The description of the wine that is sometimes found on the back label of the bottle may drastically change as the wine ages in bottle. Indeed, even as you drink wine you will notice a distinct evolution of its flavor profile. Nevertheless, it's worth noting that many wines are made ready to drink as soon as they are placed in bottle. Such wines will invariably have a short life span, which precludes them from developing much bouquet. They will be fruity, soft, and supple, and fully ready for immediate consumption.

IDENTIFYING FLAVORS

Neophytes are generally in awe when a wine maven spouts off a detailed description of the flavors found in a wine. Fledgling wine tasters have great difficulty coming up with a scant one or two flavor.

Do some people have a greater sense of smell and taste than others? The answer to this question is a qualified yes. Nevertheless, the vast majority of people have more than adequate sensory perception to be able to fully enjoy the flavors and artistry found in wine.

Can you separate the flavor of blackberries from raspberries? Do you know what kiwi and gooseberries taste like? It takes a little concentrated effort to commit these flavors to memory. In blindfold tests, many people have difficulty discerning one kind of fruit preserves from another. Often the best description they can come up with is that it is sweet, tart, and fruity. However, when they smear the preserves on a slab of toast, they see its color and texture and obviously they read the label. That's the primary reason they identify what they taste. They have great difficulty coming up with the specific flavor without the assistance of the visual sense.

The problem is most people do not recognize the flavors in wine because they have not committed the specific flavors to memory. Often sweetness is the culprit. We put sugar in coffee, we drink lemonade, and we eat strawberry jelly and apple pie. These are all exceedingly sweet substances. Even fruit in its natural form is sweet. In dry wine these fruity flavors are present with minimum amounts of sweetness. Many individuals have difficulty recognizing flavors without their associated sweetness. To commit flavors to memory, you should mentally dissect the sweetness from the fruit before inserting the specific flavor into your memory bank.

Another problem is that many tasters do not drink wine at the proper temperature. Excessively cold wines have their flavors dampened, whereas in wines that are too warm, the flavors are blurred and out of focus. The concentration of flavors increases as the temperature rises; however, after a certain point, they become out of focus and difficult to recognize. A wine that has flavors of pineapple, mango, and papaya when in focus will be smeared out at higher temperatures, and the best we may be able to discern is tropical fruit, or in the worst scenario perhaps the description may be only "fruity." Most white wine are best at around 50-55 degrees F, most reds around 60-65 degrees F.

It takes concentrated effort to commit the scents and flavors of the wonderful savors available to us, but it's well worth the effort. These sensory experiences are one of life's greatest pleasures.

CHAPTER 2
The Concept of Flavor

"This isn't wine! It tastes like lemonade."

Everyone uses the word "flavor," but few know what the word really means. Most people use "flavor" and "taste" interchangeably. However, "flavor" and "taste" are not synonyms. In the caption above, the word "tastes" is used incorrectly. **The sense of taste can only discern tart (acids), salt, sweet, bitter, and umami (savoriness).**

Taste is detected by tiny organs called taste buds. The perception of taste is more complicated than formerly thought. The mapping of taste buds on the tongue: sweet at the tip, salt just behind the tip, acids at the sides, and bitter at the back is an understatement. Granted, most of the taste buds are found on the tongue, but they are also found scattered all about the mouth, and even in the larynx and upper esophagus. The structure and function of the taste bud is also more complex than previously taught. In the traditional teachings, each of the tastes had their own specific taste buds; however, recent studies have shown this is not the case. A single taste bud may have cells within it that are receptive to a variety of taste sensations. It is the pattern of stimuli that the brain receives from the taste buds that determines what taste sensations we perceive rather than the stimulation of sets of specific cells.

TASTE + SMELL = FLAVOR

Figure 1: Flavor is an integration of the sense of smell with the sense of taste.

Flavors

When we drink lemonade, the taste buds discern sweet and tart, and the nose perceives the essence of lemon. The scent of lemon travels from the mouth up the back of the throat and into the nasal cavity; the nose smells lemon, and the taste buds determine sweet and tart. The brain receives signals from the nose and from the taste buds. It integrates the two signals together and relays to our consciousness the message: lemonade. It is important to note that the scientific meaning of taste is strictly confined to the detection of salt, sweet, tart, bitterness, and a newly discovered sensation, umami, which detects succulence. You need both the sense of taste and smell to create flavor.

Smell

The nose identifies the specific character of flavor. Chemical compounds in a wine that give rise to its scent are called **flavorful extracts**. If you bite into a ripe banana with your eyes shut, the mouth feels its smooth and soft texture, the taste buds detect its sweetness and savoriness, but it is not until the nose perceives the smell of banana that you know what you are eating. The development of flavor is the essential element in producing a quality wine. There can be little doubt that flavorful extracts are the star attractions in a wine. Although the taste sensations of acids and sweetness only fill the role of supporting cast, they are nonetheless of paramount importance in developing a wine's flavor. You cannot perceive flavor without the sense of both taste and smell.

Taste

In a purely scientific sense, the sense of taste detects only salt, sweet, tart, bitter and umami. By itself, it cannot create flavor. However, modern convention for the general public allows the word "taste" to be synonymous with the word "flavor." The major problem is purely grammatical. Taste can be used as a verb and a noun whereas flavor is strictly a noun. You can't say "This apple pie sure 'flavors' good." You need a verb: "This apple pie sure tastes good." The confusion in vocabulary occurred because the word "taste" was coined before the physiology of flavor creation was understood. You will see that in future chapters of this book, we will use "taste" to encompass the concept of flavor. I realize this notion can be somewhat confusing, but "now you know the rest of the story."

The following paragraphs outline a detailed description of the various taste sensations.

Umami

A relative newcomer to the family of taste sensations is **umami**. Umami is a Japanese word that has no direct English translation. The word connotes a meaning similar to savoriness or lushness. There is a sense of hedonism in the word "umami." Great wines at the peak of their perfection frequently have umami, as do fully ripe fruits, and certain other exquisitely seasoned foods.

Scientists from the University of Miami (Chaudhari and Roper) have identified the taste receptor for umami. These receptors are sensitive to certain amino acids, especially the flavor producing substance **monosodium glutamate (MSG).**

It was formally thought that the amino acids in wine played no role in the sensory appreciation of wine. Although it has yet to be proven, it is highly likely that amino acids are intricately associated with the development of umami in wine.

Amino acids capable of stimulating umami receptor sites are found in abundance in a variety of foods. They are especially prevalent in substances such as soy sauce, fish sauce, cheeses, sardines, mushrooms, oysters, meats, ripe fruits, and ripe vegetables. As you can see, Oriental cooking is very rich in umami producing foods.

Salt

Salt receptors are sensitive to ionic compounds, particularly the sodium ion. Salt is the only taste sensation not applicable to wines, as it plays no role in the sensory appreciation of wine. Wine does not rely on salt to develop flavor, as there is little salt in wine; rather, it uses the sensations of acids and sweet. Salt is, however, of paramount importance in developing the flavors in foods. We will also discuss the interaction of salt in food when served with wine in great detail in part two of this book: matching wine with food. The majority of salt receptors are found on the tip of the tongue.

Bitter

The **bitterness** receptors are stimulated by a variety of organic molecules, some of which are quite poisonous. Bitterness in wine is associated with tannins. Bitter tannins are usually found in cheap, pedestrian wines. Generally speaking, bitterness is not a particularly complementary taste sensation. However, in certain food items such as the curly green leaf called frisée, bitterness can be complimentary. Wines that have very high amounts of tannin at their inception have a greater chance of becoming bitter as they age. Keep in mind that the chief sensory effect of tannins is the development of astringency (dry puckered mouth), not bitterness. Astringency is a tactile sensation, not a taste sensation. Bitterness receptors are concentrated at the back of the tongue. This is usually the last sensation detected when one tastes a wine and is most noticeable in the aftertaste.

Tart

Acid receptors are located throughout the mouth, but the majority is located on the sides of the tongue. **Acids** give a wine its tartness. They are the backbone that provides structure for the other flavorful elements in wine. Tartness gives wine its vigor and vitality. A wine lacking tartness is a dull, lifeless, and insipid beverage.

If you were to add a few drops of lemon extract (the flavorful extract or scent of lemon) to a glass of water, you will smell lemons, but all that you will taste is water. Try it! There will be no flavor because there is no taste: sweet, salt, tart, bitter, and umami are not present! Add a little citric acid (the flavorless acid found in fruits) and behold, you have created the nettlesome flavor of lemon juice. Acids support flavors; indeed, they are essential to the development of flavor.

Sweet

Sweet receptors are located throughout the mouth, but are present in greatest numbers on the front part of the tongue. Sweetness and umami are the only pleasant taste sensations in wine. The receptors responsible for detecting **sweetness** are for the most part stimulated by **sugars** and **alcohols**. The first sensation one experiences when tasting a wine is sweetness, then acidity, and lastly bitterness. Only in high quality wines does the pleasant sensation of sweetness persist to the conclusion of the tasting experience. In unbalanced wines, tartness, astringency, and bitterness take over.

The primary function of sweetness in a wine is to quell the aggressiveness of acidity. In the above discussion on taste, we created the assertive flavor of lemon juice. If we now add a little sugar to the mix, we will subdue the harshness of the lemon juice and create the savory beverage, lemonade. **Sweetness balances acidity and additionally supports the development of flavor.**

Aftertaste

In good quality wines, the flavorful extracts (scents), acids, and sweetness are present in high concentrations. They coat the mouth, and persist long after the wine has been swallowed. These elements continue to stimulate the taste buds and nasal receptors allowing flavors to extend into a long and lingering aftertaste. If a sensation is pleasurable to us, the longer it lasts, the better we like it. A prolonged and pleasurable finish is a preeminent hallmark of high quality wines.

CHAPTER 3
The Components of Wine

Wine is a composite of several categories of ingredients: water, alcohol, acids, tannins, sugar, flavorful extract, amino acids and oak. They are responsible for all of the sensory characteristics of wine. The only flavor in wine not indigenous to the grape is oak, which is derived from the oak barrel in which the wine is aged and/or fermented.

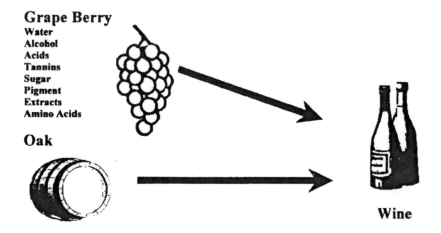

Figure 2: *The components of wine. Oak is the only ingredient in wine not derived from the grape berry itself.*

In order to understand wine, it is essential to break it down into its component parts. The quality and quantity of the parts, the structural makeup of the wine, and the artistic manner in which the parts are assembled determine the ultimate merits of a wine.

Artistry, the keynote in the creation of a quality wine, is not measurable by analyzing the chemical makeup of a wine any more than the isolated notes of a musical composition determine its merits. It is the arrangement of quality elements that generate artistry. However, before you can understand and appreciate the arrangement of the elements of a wine, which essentially equates to balance, you must first comprehend the fundamental nature and the function of its basic parts.

As you read this chapter, sip on a little wine. A glass of red and white would be ideal. Besides making you happy, you'll better understand what you read.

WATER

Water's sole purpose is to serve as the vehicle for the other ingredients in a wine. Too much water makes wine taste dilute. This occurs when significant rain falls near the time of harvest. The grapes swell with water and dilute the concentration of the extracts in the berry. This produces a larger quantity of lesser quality wine.

If the weather is ideal during the growing season and dry at the time of harvest, fully mature grapes will contain high concentrations of all the elements within the berry. Under these conditions, there is a good probability of producing high quality wine.

ALCOHOL

Mr. Al Cohol
—heavy and full-bodied

Alcohol is produced by a process called **primary fermentation**. Yeast acts like a little factory that converts fermentable grape sugars to alcohol plus additional flavorful extracts. Yeast is invariably present as a contaminant on the surface of the grape, and if allowed, fermentation will occur spontaneously once the grapes are crushed. Wines using indigenous yeast are labeled "**naturally fermented**."

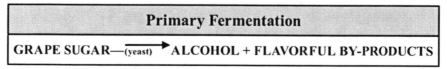

Primary Fermentation
GRAPE SUGAR—(yeast)➤ ALCOHOL + FLAVORFUL BY-PRODUCTS

Figure 3: Grape sugars are converted to alcohol plus additional flavorful extracts.

The winemaker also has the option to use special cultivated yeasts to make his wine. The same grape will produce a different wine depending on the yeast used during fermentation. The flavorful by-products produced during fermentation are unique to the specific strain of yeast and are categorized as part of the aroma of a wine.

The amount of alcohol and flavorful by-products produced during fermentation depends on the concentration of sugars within the grape berry. The riper the grape, the higher the sugars, and the greater the alcohol content will be.

Alcohol gives wine its strength and weight and is the primary ingredient that determines the body of a wine. The **body** of a wine is the feeling of weight, volume, and substance one experiences as a wine crosses your palate. Full-bodied wines have a substantive feeling on the palate. They are big, rich, and will usually have an assembly of concentrated flavorful extracts. Light-bodied wines have a more delicate, airy, and feminine nature.

We do not drink wine for its **intoxicating effects**— if that's what you're looking for, hard liquor is quicker and cheaper. The inebriating effect of wine is an annoying side effect that interferes with our perceptions. Professional wine tasters spit out their wine rather than swallowing it. Personally, I find it extremely difficult to spit out a wine that I have paid dearly for, and under ordinary circumstances, I do not routinely hold with the practice. However, when tasting a large sampling of wines, sipping and spitting is often a necessity.

Most people do not realize that **alcohol is sweet**. It is the only substance in a dry wine that directly provides sweetness. The sweetness derived from alcohol softens and rounds out the character of a wine and counters the abrasive nature of acids and tannins. Together with umami, they are the only pleasant sensation in the taste of a dry wine.

Vinosity is the term describing the agreeable warm sensation on the palate induced from a wine's alcohol content. This pleasant feeling adds character and depth to a wine. Nevertheless, too much alcohol produces a hot, biting sensation that aggressively attacks the palate. Wines that have excessive heat or have alcohol that is discernible by our sense of smell are called **alcoholic**. It is interesting to note that some wines can tolerate high alcohol levels better than others. A wine with 14.5% alcohol may have a soft, warm, pleasant feeling while a wine with 13.5% may bite with the heat of excess alcohol. The sensation elicited depends on the interactions of the other elements in the wine with its alcohol. Obviously, the higher the alcohol content, the greater the chance will be the wine will have a nettlesome alcoholic bite.

ALCOHOL
Provides weight and substance (body).
Provides sweetness.
Counters the aggressiveness of acids and tannins.
Induces intoxication.
Produces warm feeling on the palate.

ACIDS

Mr. A. Sid Sharp
thin, sharp, and angular

By itself, acidity is terribly unpleasant; it is sharp, harsh, and aggressive. High acidity makes a wine thin, sharp, and angular. Just the thought of biting into a lemon wedge or green apple can elicit its mouth-watering effect. It is not until acidity is placed in context with a wine's other elements that we can appreciate its essential nature. The chief function of acidity is to support flavors and to give structure to a wine: it is the backbone that gives sustenance to the other elements in a wine. A dry wine will be essentially flavorless without acidity. Acidity also gives wine its zing by engendering it with an appetizing, fresh, clean, crisp quality.

The predominant acid in wine is **tartaric acid**. It is a supple acid that gives ripe fruit a pleasant tartness. The harshest acid in wine is **malic acid**. Malic acid is high in unripe fruit. This acid gives green fruit its harsh unpleasant bite. Nevertheless, a little malic acid can pop up a wine's vitality by giving it a little extra vim and vigor. As the grapes ripen, the concentration of malic acid decreases and tartaric acid increases.

The winemaker can adjust the concentration of harsh malic acid by allowing a process called **malolactic fermentation** to occur. This process usually occurs spontaneously after the sugars in the must (unfermented grape juice) have been converted into alcohol through the process of primary fermentation.

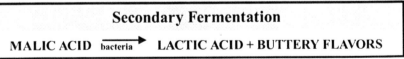

Secondary Fermentation

MALIC ACID $\xrightarrow{\text{bacteria}}$ LACTIC ACID + BUTTERY FLAVORS

Figure 4: Malolactic fermentation: Harsh malic acid is converted to softer lactic acid by the action of bacteria called the lactobacillus.

In the process of **malolactic fermentation**, also known as **secondary fermentation**, lactobacillus, a bacterial contaminant in the great majority of wines, converts tart malic acid (the same harsh acid also found in green apples) into mild lactic acid (the same soft acid that gives sour milk its mild tartness) plus a variety of flavor elements. The **buttery flavor** found in many wines (especially Chardonnay) is a by-product of malolactic fermentation. It is due to the formation of a chemical called diacetyl. If malolactic fermentation does not occur spontaneously, the winemaker can induce it by injecting the young wine with lactobacillus. The winemaker can also prevent the process from occurring by killing off the lactobacillus.

Acids lighten the weight of wines and make them less rich and more aggressive. Indeed, most high-acid wines are lightweight. However, excessive acidity gives wine a disagreeable sharp, thin, angular quality.

During a wine's maturation, its acidity declines. As a result, a youthful, tart, aggressive, red wine becomes rich, full, soft, and supple. Most high quality red wines will benefit from a little time in bottle to quell the assertiveness of its acidity. However, unless tartness is very high, a significant decline in acidity in white wines is detrimental to its character, as crisp, fresh, clean acidity is essential to the nature of most white wines.

ACIDS
Support the flavors in wine.
Make wine fresh and crisp.
Decrease the weight and richness of a wine.
Can give wine a sharp, thin, angular quality.
Decreases as wine ages.

TANNINS AND PIGMENT

Mr. Red Tannin
—a little on the rough side

Tannins are the most difficult element in wine to understand. Don't get discouraged if you don't fully grasp the topic in this section; as you read through subsequent chapters, the matter will become clear.

To experience tannin, swirl a mouthful of red wine like mouthwash. The tissues of the mouth will develop the dry, puckery feel of **astringency**—your mouth will become rough and parched and your teeth will feel dry. Tannins are only detectable in red wines; white wines have only scant amounts of tannins. Indeed, one of the major differences between red and white wines is the sensation of tannins.

Most of the tannins in wine come from grape skins. Grape varieties that have thick skins have more tannins than thinner-skinned varietals. For example, Cabernet Sauvignon, a thick-skinned grape varietal has more tannin than thinner-skinned Pinot Noir or Merlot. The high quality tannins found in premium wines come from fully ripened grape skins. Grapes not fully ripened are likely to have coarse, rough tannins.

Tannins are powerful antioxidants that preserve wine by protecting it from the harmful effects of oxygen. As you might expect, wines that are low in tannins have decreased longevity. Because of their lack of tannins, most white wines have a considerably shorter longevity than red wines.

Pigments in wine are chemical compounds called **anthocyanins**. Some of the anthocyanins in red wine bind with tannin to produce anthocyanin-tannin complexes; others remain free and unbound. As wine ages, increasing amounts of anthocyanins become bound to tannins.

Tannins represent a diverse group of compounds that bind with pigment: some tannins are small molecules, some are large, others are very large. Small anthocyanin-tannin complexes are rough, astringent, and have a red-purple color. The larger anthocyanin-tannin complexes are softer, rounder, less astringent, and have less red-purple tones and more brown tones. As wine ages, the anthocyanin-tannin complexes react with each other to form long chains. Several smaller anthocyanin-tannin complexes form fewer larger ones. Because of this effect, aging causes wine to become softer, less astringent, and browner in color.

Think of the small rough tannin-pigment complexes as unattached train boxcars. As the boxcars are added to the train, the increased load makes the train increasingly sluggish. In the same fashion, as the tannin-pigment complexes react with each other they become soft and less aggressive. If too many boxcars are added, the train will be unable to pull the load. In like manner, the anthocyanin-tannins complexes fall out of solution and become sediment. **The sediment in red wines is composed of very large anthocyanin-tannin complexes.**

Besides making a wine rough and aggressive, tannins enshroud the flavors in a wine. Think of tannins as a big furry coat wrapped around a beautiful shapely woman. You cannot appreciate the beauty beneath until she sheds her coat. In like fashion, you will not fully appreciate the flavors in a wine until it sheds some of its aggressive tannins. In a massively tannic wine, such as a young Barolo, a large percentage of the flavorful extracts are undetectable. As wine ages, however, both the amount and the astringency of tannins decrease. This allows the enshrouded flavors to gradually become uncovered and a myriad of complex flavors emerge. In a fully mature wine, flavors should be totally accessible.

There ain't any tannins here!

Another important effect of tannin is its interaction with umami. Umami accentuates the perception of tannins and they become bitter. Foods that are rich in umami, such as cheese and mushrooms clash with tannic wines—more about this later.

There are different types of tannins. Some are coarse, while others—the **noble tannins**—are fine, supple, and powdery. The skins from fully ripened, high quality grape varietals contain noble tannins. Lesser quality tannins come from pips, stems, and from the skins of unripe grapes. Oak also contains tannins. Small amounts of tannins are extracted from the wooden barrel in which wines are aged.

TANNINS
Tannins are astringent (mouth drying) compounds.
Tannins act as antioxidants that preserve wine.
Tannins represent a diverse group of compounds: some large, others small.
Tannins cover over flavors.
Anthocyanin (the wines pigment) binds with tannins.
Small anthocyanin-tannin complexes are red-purple.
Large anthocyanin-tannin complexes have associated brown tones.
The larger the anthocyanin-tannin complexes, the less astringent they become.
Umami accentuates the perception of tannins and makes them bitter.
As wine ages, the anthocyanin-tannin complexes increase in size, and the total number of anthocyanin-tannin complexes decrease in numbers.
Quality tannins come from the skins of fully ripened grapes.
The level of tannins and their astringency decrease as wine ages.

SUGAR

Miss Candy Sweet
Savory and sensuous ..."how sweet it is!"

The alcohol in dry wines generates a limited degree of sweetness. Overt sweetness is due to sugars. Sugars in a wine can either be added in the form of concentrated sweet grape juice (a procedure commonly done in Germany), or retained in the wine by stopping fermentation before all the sugars have been depleted.

Sweetness, in the form of either alcohol or sugar, counteracts the assertive qualities of acids and tannins. The aggressive tartness of acidity is tempered by sweetness. Remember how harsh lemon juice is turned to savory lemonade by adding sugar? Sugars soften a wine and make it round, soft, supple, and sensual.

SUGAR
Makes wine soft, sweet, and sensuous.
Counteracts the aggressiveness of acids and tannins.
Contribute to the body of a wine.

Sugars increase the body of a wine; however, the effect is less dramatic than that of alcohol. Alcohol and sugar have similar functions in the structural makeup of wine. They increase body, counter the aggressive attack of acids and tannins, and provide a lush and pleasant taste sensation. It is interesting to note that alcohol, the sweetening agent in dry wines, is derived from sugar.

FLAVORFUL EXTRACTS

Flavors—the star actor in the "production"
of wine

Flavors are the star actors in the "production" of wine. All of the other elements that make up wine play a supporting role to the flavorful extracts. The flavorful extracts are a wine's essence—a wine without flavors could hardly be called a wine at all.

The fruity flavors derived from the grape plus those generated during fermentation are called **aroma**. The **bouquet** of a wine represents the flavors formed as a wine ages in bottle. Flavors such as mushrooms, truffles, leather, coffee, nuts, chocolate, sandalwood, and tar are generated as wine matures in bottle. During the evolution of a wine in bottle, aroma gradually decreases and bouquet increases. Ideally, a well-constructed wine at maturity should have both aroma and a fully developed bouquet. In old wines, the fruity flavors may have completely dissipated, and all that is left is bouquet. It is difficult to identify the grape variety that produced a wine once its aroma has dissipated, as aroma is a fingerprint of the grape varietal.

Red wines have red or dark fruit flavors such as strawberries, cherries, blackberries, raspberries, and currants; white wines have white or light fleshed fruity flavors such as apples, pears, grapefruit, peaches, mangos, and lemons. There are occasional crossovers such as the black currant flavor frequently found in Sauvignon Blanc (a white wine), but red and white fruit flavors correspond predictably to the color of the wine.

Each premium grape varietal produces wine with its own distinct flavor profile: black currants in Cabernet Sauvignon, blackberries and raspberries in Zinfandel, cherries and mulberries in Merlot, and grapefruit, roses, and lychee nuts in Gewürztraminer. Other flavors intermingle in a wine's flavor profile, but specific flavor groups are typical for each particular varietal. These flavor profiles combined with other structural qualities such as the amount of acids, tannins, and alcohol, are known as the **varietal character** of the wine. Varietal character is the marker that identifies the grape variety. For example, a young Cabernet Sauvignon is full-bodied, tart, tannic, and has flavors of black currant and cedar; a young Zinfandel is full-bodied, tannic, but less tart, and has flavors of blackberries, raspberries, and black pepper.

The multiple scents and flavors comprising aroma and bouquet are called **complexity**. The greater the diversity of scents and flavors, the greater its complexity. A wine ripens just like fruit. In a well-balanced, quality wine at the peak of maturity, the concentration and complexity of the flavorful extracts should be at a maximum.

Ripe fruit flavors can give wine a sense of sweetness when in fact there are no residual sugars. The mind subconsciously associates the sweetness connected to ripe fruits with the ripe flavors found in wine.

These ripe flavors together with the sweetness derived from alcohol can give a dry wine a distinct albeit modulated sweet taste.

Flavorful Extracts
Aroma: predominantly fruity flavors.
Bouquet: predominantly non-fruity flavors.
Red wines have red or black fruit flavors: cherries, berries, black currant, etc.
White wines have light fleshed fruit flavors: apples, pears, peaches, lemons, etc.
Quality grape varietals have a specific varietal character—they are distinctive.
The concentration and complexity of flavorful extracts should be at a maximum at the peak of a wine's maturity.
Ripe fruit flavors give wine a sense of sweetness when in fact there is no residual sugar present.

OAK

A little bit of oak goes a long, long way.

Oak can be a wonderful complement to a variety of wines. Aging wines in oak barrels makes them softer, rounder, and richer. In addition, it adds both weight and an oaky flavor to wine. However, too much oak can give wine an awkward, clumsy, top-heavy feeling that can decrease complexity by covering other more delicate flavors in the wine. Oak should be used judiciously; if the flavor of oak is obvious, it is too much. After all, wine is a beverage of grapes, not wood.

A large number of diverse flavors have been said to develop from a wine's treatment with oak: some from the oak itself, others from toasted oak. These include flavors such as mushrooms, leather, spices, chocolate, caramel, honey, grass, grilled meats, nuts, and pencil shavings. The cooperage industry is the prime promoter of these claims.

Cedar is a common flavor that develops in many wines. It is especially common in Cabernet Sauvignon and Cabernet Franc. Some people have the erroneous idea that this flavor is the result of the wine being aged in cedar barrels. Cedar flavor is generated from chemical reactions within the wine itself and is not engendered by contact with cedar wood.

OAK
Makes wine richer, rounder, softer, fuller bodied, and more complex.
Too much oak decreases complexity and makes the wine clumsy and top-heavy.

Quiz

Let's see how well you have mastered this topic with a little quiz.

True or False

1. Wet weather at the time of harvest will produce dilute tasting wines.
2. Alcohol supplies the sweetness in a dry wine.
3. Tannins counteract the aggressive character of acids.
4. Acids support flavors; tannins suppress them.

5. Small amounts of oak increase complexity, large amounts decrease complexity.

6. Tannins bind with pigments to form anthocyanin-tannin complexes.

7. Large anthocyanin-tannin complexes are associated with soft, supple wines.

8. As a wine ages, acids and tannins decrease.

9. As wine ages, it becomes softer, rounder, and less astringent.

10. Small anthocyanin-tannin complexes react with each other to produce large anthocyanin tannin complexes.

11. Small anthocyanin-tannin complexes are rougher and more astringent than larger ones.

12. Oak makes a wine round, soft, and full-bodied.

13. Malolactic fermentation makes a wine less tart.

14. Malolactic fermentation produces a buttery taste in wines.

15. Malic acid is more tart than tartaric acid.

16. As wine ages, fruity flavors are replaced by flavors such as mushrooms, truffles, leather, and coffee.

17. Older wines have less bouquet and more aroma.

18. Primary fermentation changes grape sugars to alcohol and other flavors.

19. Tannins are antioxidants that preserve wine.

20. White wines have high amounts of tannins.

21. The chief function of acidity is to support flavor.

22. Ripe fruit flavors gives wine a sense of sweetness.

23. The varietal character of a wine diminishes with age.

24. Tannins are a large group of associated compounds of many sizes.

25. Lactic acid is softer and less tart than malic acid.

26. The acidity in a wine is made up of a variety of acids, the principal one of which is tartaric.

27. A dry wine without acidity would be essentially flavorless.

28. Acidity within the grape decreases with ripening.

29. Acidity within the wine decreases with aging.

30. Acids in wine together with a wine's scents produce its flavor.

31. The oak flavor in wine comes from the oak barrel in which it was aged.

32. Lactic acid has less tartness than malic acid.

33. Young wines have more fruity flavors than older wines.

34. Cabernet Sauvignon has a thicker skin than Pinot Noir.

35. Thick-skinned red grapes produce deeper pigmented wines.

36. High levels of tannins obscure the flavors in wines.

37. Flavor equals taste plus smell.

38. The cedar flavor in some wines is developed by aging wine in cedar barrels.

39. If you lose your sense of smell, you cannot distinguish flavor.

40. Umami is a taste sensation.

Answers

All are true except for number 3, 17, 20 and 38.

CHAPTER 4
Balance

*Balance is an essential element in artistry
and beauty.*

Balance can be found in abundance throughout nature. It is a quality present in all artistic works: paintings, sculptures, architecture, music, cooking, literature, and many others. It is also a fundamental concept in science: mathematics, physics, chemistry, astronomy, and biology.

Balance concerns itself with the arrangement of elements. An artist mixes his colors and strategically places his shapes on a canvas so that they are pleasing to the eye, a composer harmoniously arranges his notes, and an architect skillfully maps out his designs. The winemaker too must integrate and use to best advantage the ingredients that Mother Nature has provided for him in the grape to produce an artful, well-balanced wine.

Consider the human face. Eyes and ears are symmetrically paired and of just the right size. The nose and mouth are centered and strategically placed on the face. They aren't too large or too small—they perfectly fit the context of the face. There is a harmony in the size and placements of the facial features. Harmony creates beauty, and beauty creates pleasure.

Why would a little child be afraid of someone wearing a scary Halloween mask? That scary face has never harmed the child; she may never have seen such a face before in her entire life. So, why is there fear? The mask still has hair, two eyes, two ears, a nose, and a mouth. However, there is something wrong with that face that affects our senses. The reason for the fear is that the face is not balanced. The image on the mask has lost the sense of proportion, size, and symmetry; it is distorted; it has lost its beauty. The eyes are uneven, or too big, or small; the nose is out of proportion, or is perhaps misshaped; the lips are pursed in a crooked snarl, and the teeth are large, irregular, sharp, and threatening. In other words, the face has lost balance, and the child can sense that. The face is ugly. In its extremes, wine that has lost balance can also be ugly. An unbalanced, coarse, tannic, and harsh wine can be almost undrinkable.

Just as all of us can't have a perfect face, we can't expect all wines to be in perfect balance. In fact, just as in people, perfection is the rare exception. When balance is off just a click, a wine will not be as good as it could be; nevertheless, it may still be a wine of very high quality. Indeed, if all wines were perfect, wine tasting would lose its intrigue. The vast majorities of wines are defective in one way or the other. It is a rare wine that meets the criteria for perfection.

In a flawlessly balanced wine at maturity, all the parts of the wine are in perfect harmony, there are no excesses or deficiencies. The wine is symmetric; it has no loose ends. It is not too tart, too flat, too tannic, too drab, too oaky, too sweet, too dry, too light, too heavy, too simple, too short (aftertaste), too weak, or too strong. It is just right! It is perfectly balanced.

Wine is an anthropomorphic beverage—it's people like. It is born, matures, fades, and then dies. Like people, wines are a little rough, rambunctious, and unpolished in their youth; supple and sophisticated at maturity, and weak and feeble when they get old. Some wines have great longevity; others fade out soon after they are born.

Figure 4 The aggressiveness of acids and tannins are balanced by the gentle sweetness from alcohol and/or sugar.

Balance in wine is a multifaceted issue, and all of a wine's parts are involved. However, the principal contest is an interplay between acids and tannins—the assertive elements, and alcohol and sugar— the agreeable elements: the villains versus the good guys.

The pleasant sensation in a dry wine is sweetness, which is derived from alcohol, and the apparent sweetness associated with ripe fruity flavors. Acids are needed to bolster flavor, and tannins are required to protect wine during its aging process. In a balanced wine "at maturity," acids and tannins must be assuaged by the sweetness derived from alcohol or sugar so that the wine is supple and pleasing to drink. Moreover, this metamorphosis must occur at the specific time in the wine's life when flavorful extracts peak.

During the life history of a wine, its components are in a state of flux. A full understanding of the changes that occur as a wine evolves is essential if you are to grasp the concept of balance.

Aging in Red Wines

Because of the tannin content in red wines, there is a considerable difference in the life histories of red and white wines. Tannins give red wine greater longevity than white wines. This gives red wines time to go through a slow evolutionary change. The description of characteristics of a wine in its youth will be very different than at maturity.

In red wines, both acids and tannins decline as wine ages. Additionally, tannins become rounder, softer, and suppler—they lose their coarse, abrasive feeling. During this same time, the concentration of flavorful extracts gradually increases, and at maturity they peak for varying lengths of time before gradually beginning their decline. As flavors are evolving, aroma (fruity flavors) diminishes and bouquet increases: a myriad of exotic and complex flavors such as truffles, tobacco, chocolate, or leather develop. Following the stage of maturity, acids, tannins, and flavorful extracts gradually descend in a downward spiral. At the wine's death, acids and tannins are practically depleted and flavors have faded away.

Unlike acids and tannins, alcohol and sugar concentrations remain essentially unchanged through the entire life span of a wine. From the sensory aspect, sugars and alcohol may appear to change, but this is only an illusion. For example, a youthful Vouvray may be a very tart and dry appearing white wine even though it has residual sugars. However, as it matures, the wine progressively becomes sweeter, fuller, and richer. Sugars and alcohol have not changed, but acids have. High levels of acidity will cancel out sweetness and make a wine appear thinner than it actually is. As acids fall, sweetness and richness become more apparent, and the true nature of the wine is revealed.

Most quality red wines take time to mature. In their youth, they can be rough and unpolished. When we evaluate a young red wine for balance, we must project what the wine will be like at some time in the future. Will acids and tannins be supple when the fruit peaks? Will all of the elements of the wine be in harmony?

In a mature wine, acids should be just high enough to support the flavorful extracts. Tannins should be soft, powdery, and not interfering with the accessibility of flavors. Most young red wines destined for aging are assertive and have aggressive acids and tannins. Because acids and tannins dwindle with time, out of necessity, they must be high when the wine is young. Youthful red wines with an aggressive edge that the taster feels will be harmonious at maturity are said to be **balanced for longevity**.

Flavorful extracts in wine must keep pace with the concentration of acids and tannins. The higher the level of acids and tannins, the more fruity extract a wine must contain. If fruity flavors are deficient to begin with, they will have peaked and faded away long before acids and tannins have declined sufficiently to make the wine supple. If flavors peak before or after acids and tannins have become supple, the wine is unbalanced. As you can see, it takes an artistic hand to orchestrate a performance where acids and tannins are supple at the time when flavors peak, and the majority of wines will be off a degree or two. Defects in wine are commonly related to its balance.

As a red wine matures, it decreases in color intensity and increases in the amount of brown tones. **Oxidation** (exposure to air) is the chief factor in propelling a wine through its color changes. Oxygen "burns out" red and purple pigments and replaces them with brown tones. With time, oxygen slowly seeps into the bottle and chemically reacts with wine. To a point, this is very desirable, as oxygen is necessary for a wine to evolve; the maturation of a wine depends on oxygen. However, oxygen, the force that pushes a wine to maturity, continues to push it into its decline and ultimate death. It is becoming more apparent that it makes little difference in the manner the bottle is sealed: real cork, artificial cork, waxed over cork, or screw cap; oxygen will find its way into the wine.

It should be noted that some wines will have increasing amounts of disagreeable acidity that increases in amount with age. This is not natural acidity, rather it is the acidity of spoilage: acetic acid—vinegar. This acidity will be accompanied by the vinegary smell of ethyl acetate.

The chart below portrays the life history of a typical red wine.

THE LIFE HISTORY OF A BALANCED RED WINE			
Time →			
Young	Mature	Decline	Dead
acids	**acids**	acids	acids
tannin	**tannin**	tannin	tannin
rough	*round*	*thin*	
flavor aroma	**flavor** aroma/ bouquet	flavor bouquet	flavor
alcohol	**alcohol**	**alcohol**	**alcohol**
sugar	**sugar**	**sugar**	**sugar**
tart and rough	round, soft, silky, supple, and sophisticated	weak, flat, and flabby	oxidized
Color			
(red-purple)	*(red-purple-brown)*		*(brown)*
increasing brown tones →			
(deep)			*(light)*
decreasing color intensity →			

Figure 5: The font size indicates the concentration of the components. The fall in acids and tannins coordinates with the rise in the concentration of flavorful extracts so that at maturity, the wine is supple and flavors are at a maximum. The wine is balanced. Alcohol and sugars remain essentially unchanged during the entire life span of the wine. As wine ages, its color intensity lessens and the wine picks up brown tones.

Balance can also be demonstrated in graphic form. In the graphs below, the supple zone indicates concentration levels at which acids and tannins are soft and round, and flavors are at high levels. A wine is balanced when acids, and tannins are in the supple zone at the time when flavors peak.

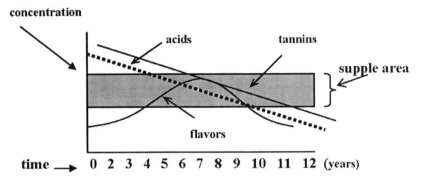

Figure 6: This graph represents a balanced wine. The wine is mature when flavors peak, at which time the acids and tannins are in the supple area. In this particular example, acids become supple at 4 years. Tannins become supple at 6 years; flavors fade away at 9 ½ years. The period of maturity extends from 6 to 9 ½ years. The wine is at peak maturity at 7 years.

Both acids and tannins should be in the supple zone at the time flavors peak. The graph below (figure 7) is an example of an unbalanced wine. In this graph, tannins are too high at the time when flavors peak. The result is a wine that is rough and astringent, and part of the flavors will be obscured by the blanketing effect of high tannins. In the case where acids are above the supple zone at the time flavors peak, the unbalanced wine will be harsh, aggressive, and overly tart.

concentration

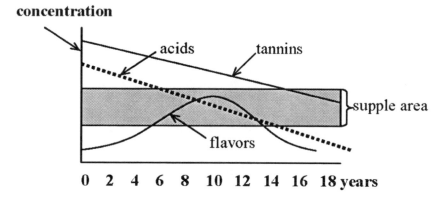

Figure 7: This is a graph of an unbalanced
wine. When flavors peak, tannin levels are not
in the supple zone, making the wine coarse,
scabrous, and out of balance.

If you have been reading carefully, you should have noticed that
alcohol and sugars are not depicted on the above graphs. However,
they are in fact represented. The level of alcohol and sugars controls
the supple zone on the graph. For example, in wines with high levels
of acids, increasing levels of alcohol or sugar must be present to
maintain balance. Without this counterbalancing effect of sweetening
agents, the wine would be overly coarse and aggressive. The levels of
acids and tannins control the area and location of the supple zone.

concentration

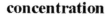

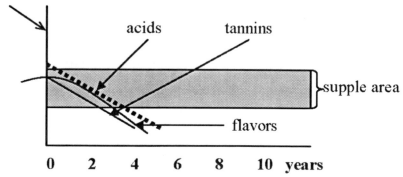

Figure 8 This is the graph of a red wine ready
to drink at the time of bottling. Fruity flavors

are in the supple zone until about 3 years of age. Acids fall out of the supple zone a little less than 4 years of age. This wine will have plenty of aroma, but little bouquet, as the wine has not had sufficient time in bottle to develop bouquet.

In figure 8 we have the graph of a red wine made to drink on release. You can see that at about 4 years of age, fruit supporting acidity wanes and the wine begins to lose flavor. This style of wine will have plenty of fruity flavors, but its short life precludes it from ever developing significant complexity. Because of low levels of tannins, the wine is also susceptible to the damaging effects of oxidation. Nevertheless, in spite of its short longevity, this style of wine can be very enjoyable and often represents good values.

When we evaluate a young wine for balance, question the level of acids, tannins, sweetening agents (sugar and/or alcohol), and flavorful extracts. At maturity, there should be just enough acidity to support flavorful extracts; tannins should be round and powdery, and flavors should be fully accessible. The wine should be soft, sophisticated, supple, and have a long, concentrated aftertaste.

It should be noted that mature, balanced wines might not be the best partners for wine-food pairings. Youthful wines with aggressive acids and tannins are frequently ideal matches for a variety of dishes. Nevertheless, some high quality, mature, umami rich wines can create scintillating symmetries when paired to similarly styled foods. Without food, however, mature, balanced, high quality wines are masterpieces in their own right. More about this in Part II of this book.

BALANCE IN RED WINES		
	Function	*Ask Yourself*
Acids	Support flavors	Will there be too little acidity at maturity to support the flavors making the wine weak, flat, and insipid; or will there be too much acidity causing the wine to be harsh and overly tart?
Tannins	Preserve wine	Are there enough tannins to protect the wine against oxidation during its evolution to maturity, or are they too high making the wine rough and lacking in flavors at the time when flavors peak?
Flavors	The essence of wine.	Will there be a good concentration of complex flavorful extracts at maturity?
Alcohol	Provides body and sweetness	Is there enough sweetness in the wine to soften the aggressiveness of the acids and tannins so that the wine will be supple at maturity? Is the body of the wine too heavy or too light?
Sugar (sweet wines only)	Provides sweetness and a modicum of body	Is there enough sweetness in the wine to soften the aggressiveness of the acids and tannins so that the wine will be supple at maturity? Or, are sugars too high causing the wine to be cloyingly sweet.

Figure 9: Criteria for balance in red wines.

White Wines

Most quality white wines are ready to drink at their inception. They have just the right amount of acidity to establish their character and support their flavorful extracts. Flavors are fully developed, and there is usually nothing to be gained by aging the wine. The only purpose of cellaring most white wines is value and availability: if the price is right, buy the wine before it is no longer available.

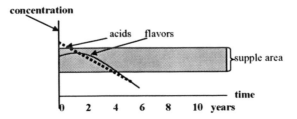

Figure 10 This is the graph of a typical white wine. At about 4 years of age, fruit supporting acidity falls out of the supple zone and the wine begins to lose its flavors. The life span of this wine is about 4 years.

The graph in figure 11 shows the features and life span of a typical white wine. This particular graph is that of a run-of-the-mill California Chardonnay. As you can see, the wine starts to fall apart after about 4 years.

There are a few white wines, such as white Burgundy, Savennières, and Vouvray, which do benefit with a little aging in bottle; however, the great majority of white wines start to decline a few years after bottling. The exceptions are wines that have high initial levels of acidity. If acids are inordinately high, a little bottle age will allow time for acids to decline and permit the wine to soften.

Because white wines have insignificant amounts of tannins, they are less protected from the devastating effects of oxidation than red wines. Longevity in white wines is therefore relatively short. Some white wines will start to decline shortly after bottling, whereas most high quality red wines need several years (some need tens of years) in bottle to mature. In outstanding years, the elite of the great reds can last for a century or more.

White wines gradually become darker in color with age. The presence of noticeable brown tones in a white wine should make one very suspicious that the wine is in decline. However, don't mistake a wine with a dark golden color for a declining wine that contains brown tones. With dry wines, darkening is not a good sign, but quality dessert wines invariably take on a dark but brilliant golden hue with age. Brilliance is the key observation. Brilliance is a sign of health for both red and white wines. A wine that sparkles as if light is being generated from within the glass is likely to be healthy. As wines decline, they lose their sparkle and become dull and lifeless. In advanced stages of deterioration, they become overtly cloudy.

Most quality white wines are balanced on release from the winery. Good levels of acidity support a complex array of fruity flavors. In balanced sweet wines, sugars supply just enough sweetness to counter acidity, but not to the extent that the wine becomes cloying.

A few white wines, such as Viognier and Gewürztraminer have only moderated levels of acidity at their inception. They do not rely on crisp acidity for their appeal; rather, their charm is evoked by the lush, rich, round, polished mouth feel that they elicit.

THE LIFE HISTORY OF A DRY WHITE WINE			
time →			
Youthful		*Declining*	*Dead*
acids	**acids**	acids	acids
flavor	**flavor**	flavor	flavor
alcohol	**alcohol**	**alcohol**	**alcohol**
sugar	**sugar**	**sugar**	**sugar**
fresh, clean, crisp, and flavorful		flat & flabby	oxidized
Color Changes			
pale to light golden		yellow-brown	brown
increasing brown tones →			
increasing color intensity →			
decreasing brilliance →			

Figure 11: The font size indicates the concentration of the components (acids, flavorful extracts, alcohol and sugar). When a white wine ages, acids decline, while alcohol and sugars remain unchanged. In most white wines, flavors are at their maximum at inception and fresh clean acidity is essential to their charm. Unlike red wines, a white wine increases in color intensity with age. In both red and white wines, brown tones increase with aging.

Although acids, tannins, and flavorful extracts are major players relating to balance, there are many others. Too much oak covers over a wine's delicate flavors and actually makes the wine less complex. Oaky wines are clumsy and top heavy. The dominance of a particular scent, such as the buttery flavor in some Chardonnays, can be inundating, and similar to ponderous oak, can obscure other more delicate scents and flavors. The character of the flavor profile should also fit the wine. For instance, tropical fruit flavors fit better in wines with restrained levels of acidity, whereas wines that abound with flavors of lemons, limes, grape fruit, and green apples work best with higher levels of crisp, clean acidity. Low acid fruity flavors (ripe flavors) do better with gentler levels of acidity.

You will discover other aspects of balance as you become more experienced in tasting wines.

Descriptions of mature wines that contain the adverb "too" are a tip-off to defects in balance: too heavy, too light, too sweet, too tart, etc. Keep in mind, however, that young, high quality red wines that have great longevity usually will have high levels of acids and tannins in their youth. It is only at maturity when acids and tannins enter the supple zone.

BALANCE IN WHITE WINES		
	Function	*Ask Yourself*
Acids	**Support flavors**	**Are acids too high making the wine tart and harsh, or are they too low causing the wine to be weak, flat, and flabby?**
Flavors	**The essence of wine**	**Is there a good infusion of concentrated and complex flavorful extract?**
Alcohol	**Major contributor to the body of a wine. Also provides sweetness in a dry wine.**	**Is there enough sweetness (derived from alcohol) in the wine to soften the aggressiveness of the acids so that the wine will be supple? Is the wine too heavy or too light?**
Sugar	**Counters the aggressiveness of acidity, provides sweetness and some weight. Gives wine a succulent, lush character.**	**Are sugars too high making the wine cloying, or are they too low causing the wine to be tart, angular, and aggressive.**

Figure 12 Criteria for balance in white wines.

Balance in Foods

Although this part of the book deals with wine, it would be incomplete to leave the topic of balance without addressing food. Balance in a food preparation implies careful planning, flawless preparation, and impeccable plating. Balanced foods are precisely seasoned, perfectly cooked, and artfully plated. Quality foods that have been exquisitely prepared and tastefully plated are the epitome of gourmet dining.

Foods are savored by four of our five senses: sight, smell, taste, and feel. Too many chefs forget about the sense of sight. They work hard preparing a great dish and then simply dump it on a plate.

A tremendous amount of the enjoyment of a dish is viewing it. In a balanced plate presentation, all of the visual elements artistically blend together. The size, color, and design of the plate fit the context of the food. Food items are spatially arranged on the plate in an artistic fashion. A skillful chef uses not only the width and breadth of the plate in his arrangement, but also stacks his foods to strengthen the impression of height. Colorful items such as fruits, vegetables, condiments, sauces, and edible flowers brighten the composition both through their vivid colors and by the artistic way they are arranged on the plate.

Foods without balance lack harmony and artistry. They have defective qualities that mar their character. Unbalanced foods are too flat, too tart, too sweet, too bland, too drab, too salty, too bitter, too runny, too mushy, too firm, too tough, too dry, too raw, too well-done, too fatty, too starchy, too rich, too lean, too heavy, too light, too spicy, too hot, too cold, etc. They are lacking in one or more aesthetic qualities.

Foods, like wines, have balance, precision, and complexity. A good dish will hold your interest because it is pleasing to the eye and has a variety of exotic scents, flavors, and textures that are delivered in an artful manner. Items are colorful, and artistically arranged. Like a piece of artwork, high quality, balanced foods gainfully stimulate the senses and generate pleasure and interest.

A balanced wine successfully paired with a balanced food is the quintessence of culinary experiences.

Quiz

True or False:

1. In a balanced red wine, tannins will be supple at the point when the wine is mature.

2. Acidity is high when a wine is young and decreases as wine ages.

3. In a balanced wine, all components are in harmony at the point of maturity.

4. As red wines age, their color intensity decreases.

5. A wine without adequate acidity will be flat, flabby, and lacking in flavor.

6. A young wine can have high levels of acids and tannins and still be in balance.

7. In a balanced red wine, flavors peak at the same time that acids and tannins become supple.

8. A wine will never be great if it lacks balance.

9. Excessive oak can throw a wine out of balance.

10. Balanced foods have all of their components in harmony; there are no excesses or deficiencies.

11. Most white wines are ready to drink at their inception.

12. White wines that have inordinately high initial levels of acidity will usually benefit from aging.

13. The chief function of acidity is to support flavor.

14. In a balanced wine at maturity, the aggressiveness of acids and tannins is exactly counterbalanced by alcohol or sugar.

15. The first taste sensation to be appreciated when one tastes a wine is bitterness.

Answers

All are correct except # 15. Bitterness is the last taste sensation to be appreciated. The first sensation is sweetness, followed by acidity.

CHAPTER 5
The Sensory Evaluation of Wine

Wine is one of the few artistic works that are evaluated by four of our five senses. In evaluating a wine, it is best to follow the sequence of sight, smell, taste, and feel in that order, as the tasting experience builds from one sense to the other.

Make sure that your wine glass is clean and free from any soapy residue, as a soapy film can seriously taint a wine. It's hard to believe, but high quality stemware will make your wine taste and smell significantly better. The best glasses are thin walled with a fine, unrolled edge and a narrow stem. Avoid tinted and etched glasses. There are several superb wine glass manufacturers available. The Riedel Company makes very high quality stemware that will show your wine at its best. It makes no sense to spend top dollars for premium wines, and then serve them in poor quality stemware.

SIGHT

Ahh...Crystal clear!

When you look at a wine, you can get a very good idea of what to expect when you sniff and sip. There are three aspects of inspection: **clarity, depth, and hue**.

When you evaluate the appearance of a wine, hold the glass against an illuminated, but not too bright, white background. Tilt the glass away from you and observe the wine from its outer edge into the bowl of the glass. The best place to evaluate the hue of a wine is along its outer edge. It is here that you will notice the changing spectrum of color as you progress from the rim into the bowl of the glass. In red wines, brown tones will first be detected along the outer rim of the wine, and adjacent to brown tones are red hues; purple tones become more dominant as you progress into the bowl. This color spectrum is found in the majority of red wines.

Clarity

All quality wines, red and white, should be crystal clear. When a wine starts to deteriorate, it loses its brilliance and ultimately becomes cloudy. A wine that has a dull sheen can nevertheless be clear. Tiny points of particulate matter are present in dull wines that are too small to be seen by the naked eye. These particles nevertheless absorb light just like tiny particles of carbon in a diamond rob it of its sheen. As the wine continues to deteriorate, the tiny points of particulate matter enlarge, and the wine becomes overtly cloudy. Cloudiness in a deteriorating wine is due to a colloidal suspension; such particles will not fall out as sediment. Don't confuse cloudiness that occurs when one stirs up the sediment of a wine with the turbidity of a deteriorating wine. Turbidity that occurs from stirred sediment will ultimately settle down, and the wine will again become clear.

A sound wine will be sparklingly clear and will appear to have light generating from within the wine itself. These scintillating light rays indicate a healthy wine that has the potential to be a wine of very high quality.

Depth of Color

Red Wines

Wine is a product of fruit. As any fruit ripens, its skins take on more pigment. The green color of unripe fruit changes to brighter colors: oranges become orange, bananas become yellow, and cherries become red. As the fruit continues to ripen, pigments continue to increase; the color of the fruit deepens, and fruit becomes sweeter, less tart, and more flavorful. It is easy to see that wines made from ripe grapes will be darker in color than wines made from less ripe grapes.

Acids in fruit decrease with ripening. If the fruit becomes too ripe, there is not enough tartness to support flavors, and the fruit becomes flat, and lackluster. With further ripening, the fresh, crisp flavors in a ripe apple begin to deteriorate: the apple becomes sweeter, but as acidity wanes, flavor flag; the apple becomes mealy, tasteless, and drab. The wine maker strives to pick his grapes at peak ripeness, but before acidity declines to levels that are not sufficient to support the development of flavor. Wines made from fully ripe grapes will have good depth of color, yet adequate acidity to support the fruity flavors. Wines lacking in depth of color are made from grapes that were not fully ripened, or from grapes that were picked during a wet harvest. Rain occurring shortly before or during harvest time will dilute the concentration of flavors, sugars, acids, and pigment within the grape resulting in a wine lacking in flavors, light in body, and lower in depth of color. Evaluating the depth of color in a red wine can tell us a great deal about its character, and the key to this equation directly correlates to the ripeness of the grape berry.

Evaluating Color

Each grape variety is gifted with its own assemblage of genetic traits that dictate its development. Some grape varieties will produce deeply pigmented wines; others will produce less pigmented wines. When you evaluate a wine for depth of color, you must stay within the confines of the same grape variety. Because of their genetic make-up, each grape variety will be limited to a given spectrum of color intensity. You cannot compare the color of Cabernet Sauvignon with Pinot Noir, or Bordeaux with Burgundy, or a Zinfandel with a Merlot and draw any significant conclusion in regard to quality. That being said, you can learn a great deal about a wine just by evaluating its color.

Acidity

You would expect that wines made from deeply pigmented ripe grapes would have less acidity that those made from less ripe grapes. However, it is common practice to add tartaric acid to wines that the wine maker feels are deficient in acidity for the particular style of wine that he is creating. Unfortunately, such ministrations can adversely affect the longevity and ultimate quality of the wine. It is therefore entirely possible that a deeper pigmented wine will have more acidity than a less pigmented wine. Therefore, acidity in a wine might not related to its depth of color

Alcohol

Alcohol in wine is formed by the fermentation of sugar. The riper the grape, the more pigment it will contain, the more sugar it will contain, and the higher the alcohol content will be in the resulting wine. Therefore, it is logical to conclude that **deeper colored wines are likely to have greater alcohol content.**

Alcohol gives wine strength, sweetness, weight, and richness. Indeed, alcohol is responsible in great part for the body of a wine. Wines with little body feel light, weak, and dilute; whereas full-bodied wines are likely to be rich, heavy, strong, and concentrated. Because of high alcohol levels, **deeply pigmented wines will likely have a rich, full body**.

Tannins

Quality tannins are obtained from the thickened skins of fully ripened grapes. Ripening causes the grape skin to thicken—**the riper the grape, the thicker it's skin, and the greater its concentration of both pigment and tannin**. More aggressive tannins are derived from grape stems and pips.

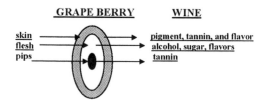

Figure 13 Pigment and tannins and some

> *flavor come from the grape skin; acids, sugars*
> *and flavorful extracts come from the flesh*
> *of the grape berry. Pips and stems provide*
> *rough tannins. Grape juice becomes wine*
> *when sugars ferment to produce alcohol plus*
> *additional flavorful extracts.*

Flavors

It is obvious that flavors develop with ripening of the grape, and the riper the berry the more pigmented the wine. Wines made from fully ripened grapes will be more flavorful than those made from less ripe grapes. Therefore, deeply pigmented wines will likely have more flavor than less pigmented wines.

Scent

It is interesting to note that rich, full-bodied wines might not have more aroma and bouquet than less heavy wines. For some mysterious reason, light, feminine styled wines often have a greater scent than big massive wines. There are many exceptions to this statement, but it holds true more often than not.

Longevity

Because of its increased tannin content, **deeply pigmented wines will have a tendency to greater longevity than its less pigmented siblings**. The chief objection to this claim relates to those red wines that are purposely constructed for early consumption. Some of these wines can be deeply pigmented indeed; however, the structural make up of the wine precludes longevity. They are designed to be supple wines that have low levels of soft tannins, moderated acidity, and abundant amounts of rich, ripe fruity flavors. There is copious aroma, but little bouquet.

Quality

From the above scenario, it follows that wines with high pigment concentration will have more alcohol, flavors, richness, and body than lesser pigmented wines. Wines with these sensory characteristics will therefore have the potential to be of high quality. These sensory qualities are tied to the depth of color of the wine. Therefore, it follows that **deeply pigmented wines are likely to be of higher quality** than their less pigmented siblings. Unfortunately, properties such as balance, finesse, and sophistication are not reflected in the appearance of a wine. For this we need the sense of smell and taste.

If one were to line up a series of Bordeaux wines from the same district and from the same year, the darker colored wines would likely be the better wines. Such wines are likely to be stuffed with the ingredients necessary to make high quality wines.

The colors in wine go through a series of changes with age. **As red wine ages, its depth of color lessens and its hue changes**. This is due to the strong association of the pigments of a wine with its tannins—more about this later.

The chart below outlines the predicted characteristics of a wine as a function of its depth of color. Keep in mind that these are generalized concepts. Some wines may not follow along the lines we have illustrated below. Indeed, there are some very high quality wines that are intentionally constructed to be light, feminine, and delicate. Nevertheless, in the majority of dry reds, these constructs are valid.

DEPTH – RED WINES	
HIGH PIGMENT	*LOW PIGMENT*
high alcohol	low alcohol
full-body	light-body
richly flavored	lightly flavored
more tannic	less tannic
sweeter	drier
less nose	more nose
higher quality	lower quality
greater longevity	shorter longevity

White Wines

As a white grape ripens, it becomes deeper and more golden in color. This color is reflected in the color of the wine. Deeper colored wines are made from riper fruit than lighter colored wines. They will therefore have more sugars (and subsequently more alcohol if fermented to dry) and less acidity.

Deeper colored white wines are likely to be richer, fuller bodied, higher in alcohol, and lower in acidity than lighter colored wines. Because of their higher levels of alcohol and the ripe character of their fruit, they have some sweetness in spite of the fact that there may be no residual sugars.

Lightly pigmented white wine will likely have high levels of clean, crisp, acidity and lower levels of alcohol. They will have a lighter body and will be more delicately flavored. The lightness, subtleties, and precision in these wines are part of their charm. There are many outstanding wines that have a light color: Chablis and

Mosel-Saar-Ruwer wines are prime examples. The **color in a dry white wine is not a predictor of quality**.

In dessert wines, color is a predictor of quality. This is because dessert wines are dependent upon sugar content, which in turn is dependent on the ripeness of the grape. Quality dessert wines will have greater depth of color that increases in depth with age.

DEPTH – DRY WHITE WINES	
HIGH PIGMENT	**LOW PIGMENT**
high alcohol	low alcohol
fuller bodied	lighter body
rich flavor	delicate flavor
less tart	more tart
more sweetness	less sweetness
DEPTH—DESSERT WINES	
higher quality in dessert wines	lesser quality in dessert wine
Depth of color is not a predictor of quality in dry white wines	

Hue

Red Wines

The pigments of red wine are intricately associated with its tannins. The raw pigments in wines are a group of compounds called **anthocyanins**. In a young wine, a sizable portion of these pigments is unbound. These **unbound pigments are red colored in tart wines and purple colored in less tart wines**. As the wine ages, the unbound pigments attach themselves to tannins to form pigment-tannin (anthocyanin-tannin) complexes. These complexes polymerize—that is, they bind together to form larger and larger molecules. Ultimately, they become so large that they can no longer stay in solution and fall out as sediment. This reduces both the tannin and pigment concentration in the wine—the wine's color becomes less dense and astringency lessens.

As the pigment-tannin complexes polymerize, they become browner in color. Several smaller red-purple colored complexes form fewer, but larger red-purple-brown colored complexes. **The larger the complexes become, the less aggressive they become.** The wine's hue picks up progressively more brown tones as larger and larger complexes are formed. In other words, **wine becomes lighter in color, browner in hue, and suppler as it ages.**

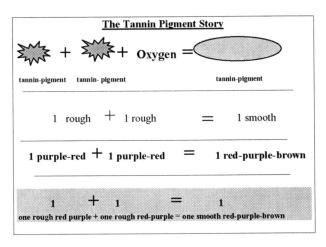

Figure 14: The many red-purple, rough and angular astringent tannin-pigment complexes become the few smooth, red-purple-brown tannin pigment complexes. Color intensity decreases and brown tones increase as a wine ages. Oxygen is used up in the process.

A summary of all this technical stuff will help clarify:

As red wine ages, it decreases in color intensity, picks up brown tones, and becomes smoother, less tart and less astringent. With age, the hue of a wine progressively changes from a youthful purple-red hue, to ruby, then brick red, then mahogany, and in the end to a tea-colored brown. The linking together of tannins requires oxygen. This oxidative force fuels the linking together of the anthocyanin-tannin complexes. This is how tannins protect a wine from the harmful effects of oxidation. The linking process uses up oxygen before it can attack the alcohol and flavor producing elements. This linkage decreases the total number of tannin-anthocyanin molecules (the many smaller become the fewer larger), which lessens the depth of color and the astringency of the wine. The onset of brown tones in most wines is a signal that the wine is either at or approaching maturity. Too many brown tones indicate a wine in decline. Remember, the best place to evaluate brown tones is at the outer edge of a forward tilted glass of wine.

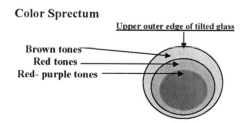

Figure 15 In a mature wine, brown tones are at the edge of the tilted glass, then, as you progress to the center of the bowl, a band of red tones is followed by red- purple tones.

White Wines

Because white wines have essentially no tannins, we are spared of all the complex mishmash that occurs in red wines. Simply stated, **white wines pick up brown tones as they age, and unlike red wines, become deeper in color.**

The perception of brown tones in a dry white wine is invariably associated with a decline in the quality of that wine. Brown tones are due to oxidation—the result of air slowly finding its way into the contents of the bottle. As wine ages, its brilliance gradually dwindles and in full decline, it becomes lackluster, dull, and possibly cloudy.

Quality sweet wines become darker in color as they age; however, the initial hue change is that of an old gold color—not brown. Sound dessert wines will be brilliant and sparkling. Some sweet wines can have great longevity and can become surprisingly dark in color. As long as the wine remains brilliant, it is likely to be sound even with a hue the shade of honey. As the wine start in its decline, it will progressively pick up dreary brown tones and lose its sparkle.

SMELL

Ahh...a profoundly complex nose!

Wine tasters refer to the scents given off by a wine as "**nose**." The sense of smell determines the specific character of the flavors— lemons, apricot, cedar, coffee and the like. You will recall that taste detects only sensations of tart, sweet, bitter, salt, and savoriness. Most scents are formed by a varied group of organic compounds (alcohols, aldehydes, esters, etc) that are present in very specific proportions. Change the proportions of these compounds and you will form totally different scents. The compounds organized in one proportion may smell like truffles, but at a different proportion these same chemicals may smell like sauerkraut.

Nevertheless, there may also be scents that are due to one specific chemical. For example, the scent of butter is due to an organic chemical formed during malolactic fermentation called diacetyl.

In a quality wine, there are multiple scents that change during the tasting experience. When you first smell a wine, you might detect the scents of blackberries, currants, and cedar; several minutes later, the scents of mushrooms and truffles might develop. As the wine sits in the glass, new and different scents are given off. The more volatile scents make the first impression; when these have blown off, less volatile scents evolve. New and different scents are also generated through chemical reactions within the wine as it aerates in the glass.

Before you smell a wine, give the glass a gentle swirl. Keeping the base of the glass on the table while swirling will help prevent spilling. This process will help to release the volatile essences within the wine. Place your nose just above the glass and take short quick sniffs in and out of your nose. Your first impressions are the most accurate as the nasal receptors quickly become refractory to specific scents. After just a few seconds of sniffing, the olfactory system (organ of smell) will begin to shut down to a particular scent. Set the glass down for a minute or two to let your nose recover, and then recheck the scent if you wish. People who have their nose continually stuck in a wine glass will appreciate very little. This is the sure sign of a novice.

A quality wine will have a plethora of exotic, complex scents that fit the context of the wine style. The scent should be typical for the varietal, and there should be no distasteful chemical or bacterial odors. The dominance of a single potent scent, such as butter or oak, will obscure other more delicate scents in the wine, thereby decreasing its complexity.

OFF-SCENTS

There are a many disagreeable scents that can be present in wine, which are due to a multiplicity of causes. The chart below is a summary of the more common off-scents and scents that dominate the character of the wine.

Off-scents	
EFFECT	**CAUSE**
Vinegar	Wine spoiled by exposure to too much air in the presence of a specific bacteria (acetobacter)
Old dank sherry smell	Oxidation of ethyl alcohol to acetaldehyde
Moldy, dank, earthy basement or wet cardboard smell.	Moldy cork—"corked wine" The mold produces a chemical called trichloroanisole (TCA) which gives the wine its dank, moldy odor.
Cheese, sour milk	Disease due to lactic bacteria (lactobacillus)
Ammonia, barnyard scents, feces, mouse droppings	Disease caused by a yeast (brettanomyces) or bacteria (lactobacillus). The defect is called brett or mousiness.
Burnt match odor	Excessive use of the sulfur (used in vineyards and wineries to prevent disease)
Rotten eggs	Excessive use of sulfur
Burnt rubber, feces, garlic, onions, rotten meat, raw onions	Mercaptans—a stable sulfur compound caused by the use of excess sulfur, or from a wine left too long on its lees (barrel sediment)
Dominating Scents	
Prunes or raisins	Wine made from overripe grapes or from grapes that were baked in the sun

Vegetal flavors	Wines made from under-ripe grapes
Woody flavors	Excessive use of oak
Excessive buttery flavor	Uncontrolled malolactic fermentation (lactobacillus)

TASTE

Ahhh...The nectar of the Gods!

When we evaluate a wine for taste, we are evaluating the performance of acids, tannins, sugars, and flavorful extracts. Strictly speaking, the flavorful extracts are more aptly expressed under the category of smell; however, as we are evaluating wine as it crosses the palate, we will address them under the category of taste. Often, the flavors that are generated in the mouth do not completely parallel those scents experienced under the category of smell. As the wine heats up in the mouth, the volatility of the various flavor producing compounds changes, and different flavors are often generated.

In a well-constructed wine, acids, tannins, flavorful extracts, and sweetness should be in perfect harmony at the peak of maturity, and the flavors generated should be in concentrations befitting the character of the wine. If the framework of the wine is lightweight, the flavors should be delicate and elegant, and if the wine is constructed on a more substantial foundation, the flavors should be big, bold, and concentrated.

Complexity is a hallmark of high quality wines. Complex wines are gifted with an array of exotic scents and flavors that continue to evolve and change during the entire tasting experience. It is this compounding into layers upon layers of changing flavors that gives a wine its intrigue and generates pleasure. There is not just one flavor, such as the lemon flavor in "Seven-Up," or the grapefruit flavor in "Squirt," but a covey of intriguing savors that continue to change as the wine sits in the glass. A single wine might have flavors of berries, cherries, cedar, truffles, licorice, chocolate, coffee, mushrooms, flowers, smoke, spices, and herbs.

The finish of the wine is the ethereal part of the wine tasting experience. Once a high quality wine is swallowed, a fanfare of exotic flavors continues to linger in a titillating dance on the palate. You do not have to be an expert to be able to experience a wine's finish—if it's good, you will know it immediately, and the longer it lingers, the better the quality of the wine. The finish of a wine is what gives it stature. Of all the attributes of a wine, **the conclusion is the best indicator of quality**, because to have a good finish, all of the other attributes have to be in tune. The wine must be concentrated, complex, balanced, and free from obvious defects to have a pleasant and savory aftertaste. Wines that are short in their finish are also short in their pleasure.

The aftertaste is a window into the character of a wine. If the aftertaste is clean, concentrated, complex, savory, sophisticated, and prolonged, you can be assured that the wine you taste is of high quality. If you learn nothing else in the chapter, remember this: Swallow the wine. Do you like the flavors? Is there complexity? Is there balance? How long do the flavors linger in your mouth? The greater the complexity, and the longer the flavors linger, the better the wine. If something gives you pleasure, the longer it lasts, the better you like it.

There is but one caveat, many high quality wines in their juvenile stage may have their flavors incompletely developed or excess tannins may obscure them. It takes experience to predict the ultimate outcome of such wines.

FEEL

Rahhh...Too damned tannic!

Most people do not think of wine as having a sensation of touch. However, the feeling of a wine as it touches the mucus membranes of the mouth is an extremely important part of the wine tasting experience. In some wines it is of paramount importance. Indeed, the quality of Champagne is dependent on the character of its mousse (the bubbles). The round, creamy feeling of a dry Champagne's mousse is the only characteristic that counters the harsh tartness of its still wine. Inexpensive Champagnes have an explosion of large coarse bubbles—like that of soda pop— that tend to exaggerate the tart aggressiveness of the still wine. However, quality Champagne will have a creamy mouth feel due to evenly spaced tiny pinpoint carbonation—like the bubbles in whipped cream.

Other tactile sensations include the dry puckery feel of tannins, the soothing viscosity of rich, fat, full-bodied wines, the mouthwatering effect of high acidity, and the heat generated in the mouth from wines with high alcohol. The briary (aggressive and spicy) feel from a young Zinfandel is one of its most appealing attributes.

Most people do not realize that the nose also has a sense of feel. The bite in the nose from high alcohol or sulfur dioxide (both found in wines) and the hot sting from hot pepper sauce are tactile sensations that can be experienced in the nose.

TACTILE SENSATIONS	
CAUSE	**EFFECT**
High tannin	Coarse, rough astringency
High acids	Sharp, aggressive, sensation that provokes a mouth-watering effect
High alcohol	Oily feeling of viscosity
High alcohol	Warm or hot mouth feel; hot biting sensation in the nose
Mousse from quality Champagne	Creamy sensation
Mousse from cheap Champagne	Rough, coarse, carbonation that accentuates harshness
Sulfur dioxide	Biting sensation in the nose

Quiz

Multiple choice:

Don't feel bad if you miss some of these questions. They are meant to be a learning experience as well as a quiz. The questions will demonstrate the practical side of what you have learned. There may be more than one correct choice. The correct answers with an explanation follow the quiz.

1. Young Beaujolais has a dominance of red tones at the edge of a tipped glass of wine, whereas mature Bordeaux has an influx of brown tones, and young Zinfandel is rich in purple tones. By evaluating color, which wine would you expect to have more tartness (acidity)? (a) mature Bordeaux, (b) young Zinfandel, (c) young Beaujolais, (d) Beaujolais and Zinfandel would have equal tartness.

2. In a young Cabernet Sauvignon (red wine) you would expect (a) low levels of tannins. (b) low levels of acidity. (c) the wine to be astringent. (d) a round, soft, smooth, sophisticated wine

3. You have before you two glasses of red Bordeaux wines from the <u>same year</u>. Wine "A" has a greater depth of color than wine "B" as well as red-purple tones at the edge of the tipped glass. There are no brown tones in wine "A", but wine "B" has a ruby edge with a small influx of brown tones. (a) Wine A is likely to be of higher quality than wine B. (b) Wine B would most likely be the most enjoyable. (c) Wine A would likely have the greater longevity. (d) All are correct.

4. You have before you a glass of high quality, fully matured white Burgundy (Chardonnay based wine). Which of the following is <u>not</u> a correct statement? (a) It will have a fruity taste. (b) If it underwent malolactic fermentation, it could have a flavor of butter. (c) It most likely did not undergo primary fermentation. (d) It should be crystal clear and brilliant.

5. You have poured before you two red Burgundy wines; both have the <u>same depth of color</u>. Wine "C" has brown tones at the edge. Wine "D" is purple at the edge with no brown tones. Both are crystal clear and have a beautiful Burgundy hue. (a)

You would expect "C" to be the older wine. (b) You would expect "C" to be of higher quality than "D." (c) You would expect "C" to be the more enjoyable of the two at the present time. (d) All are correct

6. A one-year-old Vouvray (white wine) will (a) likely have high levels of acidity. (b) have umami. (c) require a few years in bottle to reach maturity. (d) not be balanced, as it is likely to be too tart.

7. You have sitting in front of you two glasses of California Sauvignon Blanc (white wine). The glass designated X is clear, but is lacking in sparkle—it is somewhat dull appearing. The glass designated Y is lighter and radiates crystal clear. (a) "X" is likely to have more fruity flavors than "Y." (b) "X" will likely have clean crisp acidity. (c) "X" is likely to have associated brown tones. (d) "Y" is likely to be in decline.

8. You carefully pour a glass of eight-year-old Cabernet Sauvignon taking care not to disturb the sediment. You note that the wine is cloudy and has abundant brown tones. You would suspect that (a) With time, the turbidity would clear. (b) The wine is not mature; you have opened the bottle too soon. (c) The wine is likely spoiled or is in decline. (d) Although the wine is turbid, it will taste just fine.

9. A 1-year-old perfectly balanced quality Riesling Kabinett (sweet white wine) will (a) be rich in fruity flavors. (b) require several more years for it to mature. (c) be deficient in acids. (d) have soft, round, supple tannins.

10. Zinfandel (red wine) will likely have an aroma of (a) apples, lemons, and grapefruit. (b) blackberries, and raspberries. (c) tropical fruits. (d) pears, apricots, and peaches. (e) None of the above.

11. You have sitting before you two different young California Merlot wines from the same year. Wine "A" is darker in color than wine "B." You would suspect that (a) "A" is the tarter of the two. (b) "A" has more alcohol that "B." (c) "A" has less fruity flavor than "B." (d) "A" has less tannin than "B."

12. As white wine ages, (a) it gets lighter in color. (b) it gets darker in color. (c) it picks up brown tones. (d) it loses its sparkle.

Answers

1. (c) Beaujolais: The unbound pigments (anthocyanins) in wine are red colored in a high acid wines and purple colored in wines with restrained acidity. Beaujolais would therefore have a higher level of acidity than the Zinfandel. The brown tones in the Bordeaux wine indicate a wine at maturity where acidity is likely subdued.

2. (c) You would expect the Cabernet to be astringent. Young wines will be more aggressive than mature wines and have high levels of acids and astringent tannins.

3. (d) All are correct: Wine "A" has a greater depth of color, which would indicate a wine of suspected higher quality than a wine with a lesser depth of color—wine "B." The red-purple tones in wine "A" suggest that the wine is not yet near mature and will therefore have a greater longevity than wine "B" whose brown tones indicate a wine at or approaching maturity. Wine "B" will likely be the more enjoyable wine, as it is mature or at least approaching maturity. Although chronologically both wines are the same age, physiologically they are not. Wine B is precocious. It is ready sooner, will die quicker, and will probably not reach the level of quality of wine "A."

4. (a) and (c): Trick question! Don't confuse the words taste with flavor. You do not taste fruit—you taste acid and sweet; however, Chardonnay has a fruity *flavor*. OK, I know what you are thinking, current usage equates the words taste and flavor. Just checking up on you! (c) is blatantly wrong. A beverage will not become a wine until it undergoes primary fermentation: the conversion of sugars to alcohol.

5. (d) All are correct: Because of the brown tones, wine "C" is likely to be the older wine. Although both wines have the same depth of color, wine C is probably the better wine because in

its younger days—before it developed brown tones—it was darker in color: remember, as red wine ages, it loses depth of color. Darker colored wines are likely to be of higher quality then those of lighter color. Because brown tones are a sign of maturity, wine "C" is likely to be the more enjoyable of the two wines.

6. (a) and (c): Vouvray is one of those unusual white wines that, because of its high acidity, benefits from aging. The high levels of acidity do not preclude the wine from being in balance. Remember, a wine is balanced when we determine that at *maturity* all elements will be harmonious. This young, tart Vouvray is not yet mature.

7. (c) "X" is likely to have associated brown tones: A wine that has lost its sparkle is probably in decline. In such a wine, acids are likely to be low making the wine taste flat and lacking in crispness. A word of warning: some wines in decline will be spoiled and develop a vinegary bite. In such cases the wine will have high levels of unpleasant, harsh acidity—not crisp, clean acidity. Wines in decline pick up brown tones; indeed, a white wine with brown tones is invariably breaking-up.

8. (c): A turbid wine with brown tones is assuredly in decline. There is one caveat: an occasional wine that is not filtered can be sound, and still be cloudy.

9. (a): Young German Rieslings have a good bolt of lively acidity that perfectly fits the context of the wine. They are ready to drink when bottled and will not improve. The exception to this statement is that the very sweet dessert styled wines can improve with age. Remember, young wines have more acidity and fruity flavors than older wines; white wines have no perceptible tannins; most white wines are ready to drink as soon as they are bottled.

10. (b): Zinfandel will have an aroma of blackberries and raspberries. Red wines invariably have red or black colored fruit flavors.

11. (b): Dark colored wines are made from fully ripened grapes. Because they are ripe, they will be high in sugars and flavorful extracts, and rich in tannins and pigment. Wines made from these grapes will have moderated levels of acidity and high levels of pigment, tannin, flavors, and alcohol. Lighter colored wines are made from grapes that are not fully ripened. Therefore, they will be tarter and have less sugar (and subsequently less alcohol), tannins, and flavorful extract than fully ripened grapes. Although you would expect darker colored wines to have moderated levels of acidity, it is common practice to add tartaric acid to wines that are deficient in acidity, so it is entirely possible for a wine made from ripe grapes to have more acidity than a wine made from unripe grapes.

12. (b), (c), (d) White wines get darker, duller, and pick up brown tones as they age.

CHAPTER 6
Grape Varietals

There are a plethora of different grape varietals, but only a relative few are capable of making high quality wines. This chapter will cover a selected group of the more common varietals.

As the character of a wine resulting from specific varietals can vary depending on soil, climate, weather, rootstock, clone type, and the skill of the winemaker, we can only describe *typical* characteristics to look for from quality producers in good years.

The charts given at the end of each wine description are a summary of the salient features of the varietal. The "Quality" category is a generalization that characterizes the varietal's typical performance. Under the "Location" category, only the more common localities where the grape is successfully grown will be listed. Because the structural elements of a wine (acids, tannins flavorful extracts) change with age, the descriptions under "Profile" are understood to be those of young quality wines.

Use this section as a reference. When you go to a wine tasting, look up the wine's characteristics beforehand so that you will know what to expect when you sip and smell. Quality varietals will have characteristics that make them unique. Besides deriving a greater appreciation for the wines at the tasting, you are much more likely to remember the wine's salient characteristics.

Reading about a wine without tasting is pure drudgery. So, don't bore yourself. Pour yourself a glass of the same wine you are reading about. You'll be a much happier reader. What's more, you'll remember what you read.

RED WINES

Cabernet Sauvignon

This grape is unquestionably the greatest of the red wine varietals, as it consistently produces high quality wines in locations throughout the word. In California, Cabernet Sauvignon is the supreme red grape varietal, and in the Médoc region of Bordeaux, it is the dominant varietal in a large percentage of the blends. Many of the great Bordeaux wines, such a Château Latour, Château Lafite Rothschild, and Château Mouton Rothschild, have a high percentage of Cabernet Sauvignon in their blend.

California produces blended wines structured similar to those of Bordeaux that are marketed under the label of **Meritage** (pronounced like heritage). These are blends composed of Cabernet Sauvignon together with varying proportions of Merlot, Cabernet Franc, Malbec, and Petit Verdot. Some of these blends are of superb quality and can compete with the great wines from Bordeaux; however, most will have shorter longevities.

Cabernet Sauvignon is a sophisticated and powerful wine that becomes richer and more complex as it matures. It is a full-bodied wine with solid levels of tannins and plentiful amounts of acidity that support a variety of concentrated varietal flavors.

Profile Cabernet Sauvignon	
Color	Deep
Acids	High
Tannins	High
Alcohol	High
Flavors	*Aroma*: black currants, black cherries, plums, berries, cedar, mint, pepper, anise, *Bouquet*: scorched earth, tobacco, chocolate, coffee, truffles, mushrooms, pencil shavings, minerals
Quality	Very high
Locations	Worldwide
Fame	Bordeaux (France), California. However the popularity of this grape is growing worldwide.
Longevity	In California, most are best when 6-8 years old, but some can last for decades. Top quality Bordeaux wines can have tremendous longevity; some can last for a hundred years or more. There is a trend to produce French wines that mature sooner but have shorter longevity.

Regional Characteristics	
California	Fruity, powerful, rich, tart, and tannic; more concentrated but less complexity than Bordeaux. Wines are reader sooner, but have shorter longevity than Bordeaux wines.
Washington	Intensely fruity wines, but slightly less powerful than those from California. Longevity typically shorter than California.
Bordeaux	Generally less powerful and less fruity than California wines, but more elegant, complex, and introspective. However, wines from quality producers in good years may be difficult to differentiate from high quality California Cabernet.
Australia	Fruity, rich, and concentrated, but have a tendency be lacking in natural acidity.
South America	Lighter and less sophisticated than California, but otherwise similar. High-end Chilean wines can be outstanding and difficult to differentiate from California wines. Chilean wines generally are ready to drink sooner and have shorter longevity than California wines.
Italy	Cabernet based super Tuscan wines can be outstanding: rich, powerful, and complex. Wines from lesser regions are often light, tart, and lack concentration and complexity.

Gamay

The fame for this grape is in the production of the extremely popular and easy drinking Beaujolais wines. These are not sophisticated wines. However, they are loaded with ripe, raw, juicy, fruity flavors that are supported by fresh, crisp, lively acidity. The best Beaujolais wines come from a selected group of French villages after which they are named: **Brouilly, Côte de Brouilly, Régnié, Morgon, Chiroubles, Fleurie, Moulin-à-Vent, Chénas, Juliénas, and Saint Amour.** Similar (but not nearly as good) wines from

California are labeled simply Gamay. Wines labeled Napa Gamay and Gamay Beaujolais are often confused with California Gamay; however, they are not made from the Gamay grape.

Beaujolais is not a contemplative wine. Rather, it is a sound, easy drinking, and thoroughly enjoyable wine. Enjoy Beaujolais as quaffing wines, drink them at picnics or other informal occasions, or serve them along with simple everyday foods. Nevertheless, their crisp acidity and rich flavors will also complement a variety of upscale foods. To appreciate Beaujolais' great vitality, and lively, fresh, fruity flavors, drink them young.

Profile Gamay	
Color	Light to medium
Acids	High
Tannins	Low
Alcohol	Variable: 12-14%
Flavors	Spices, strawberries, raspberries, cherries, cassis, plums peaches, apricots, bubblegum, flowers
Quality	Good
Locations	Beaujolais, France
Fame	Beaujolais, France
Longevity	Short: best drunk within 1-3 years. Morgon and Moulin-à-Vent can last several years longer.

Merlot

This grape is found in the blend of almost every Château in Bordeaux. In California it is blended, but also bottled as a pure varietal. California Merlots are generally good solid wines, but they fall short of being great.

Merlot reaches its crescendo in the French village of Pomerol. Here, the celebrated and profoundly rich wines from Château Pétrus demand the highest price of all of the Bordeaux wines. The grape is grown successfully in many regions around the world, but the wines seldom reach the heights of those from Pomerol.

Because of moderation in the levels of acids and tannins, the wine is softer, rounder, and sooner approachable than Cabernet Sauvignon. However, Merlot lacks the zing and rich sturdy framework of a good Cabernet.

Profile Merlot	
Color	Moderate to deep
Acids	Moderate
Tannins	Moderate
Alcohol	High
Flavors	*French*: mulberry, black currant, plumbs. *California*: herbs, black cherry, plums. *Bouquet*: tobacco, truffles, tar, leather, cedar, chocolate, and minerals.
Quality	Medium-high
Locations	Worldwide
Fame	Bordeaux
Longevity	Variable. In California, most should be drunk within 6-7 years. High quality wines from Bordeaux can last for decades.

Nebbiolo

The quintessence of this varietal is found in Italy; here the grape produces distinguished wines of outstanding quality. The two standouts are Barolo and Barbaresco. These are big, powerful, masculine styled wines that are extremely aggressive and tough in their youth. At their inception, tannins and acids are so high that many of the wines are nearly undrinkable. Nevertheless, at maturity they are phenomenal wines with great richness, concentration, and complexity. Many consider Barolo to be the most powerful wine in the world.

Gattinara, Spanna, Inferno, and, Carema are lighter and less prestigious examples of Italian Nebbiolo wines.

Profile Nebbiolo	
Color	Deep
Acids	High
Tannins	Very high
Alcohol	High (In Italy, the legal minimum alcohol is 13%.)
Flavors	Black cherry, prunes, truffles, tar, spices, licorice, smoke, earth, leather, coffee, chocolate, faded roses, violets
Quality	High in Italy (California Nebbiolo wines are no better than average)
Locations	Italy
Fame	Italy: Barolo, Barbaresco
Longevity	High quality Barolo and Barbaresco can last for decades.

Pinot Noir

This is the celebrated grape varietal that produces the spectacular red Burgundies wines from the Côte D'Or in the Burgundy region of France. At their best, these wines are peerless. They have great breeding, incredible finesse, and their soft, elegant, and sophisticated nature makes them eminently drinkable. Burgundy's stunning array of incredibility complex and exotic savors are unique and unmatched anywhere in the world. Most of the Pinot Noir wines from regions outside of Burgundy fail to exhibit the exoticism, recherché, and complexity of those from Burgundy. However, the quality gap is rapidly closing as other countries continue to improve their skills in mastering the complexities of this varietal. California and Oregon are prime examples of locals that have made steady progress in working with this varietal; many of their wines are indistinguishable from Burgundy wines.

Profile Pinot Noir	
Color	Moderately deep
Acids	Moderate
Tannins	Moderate—soft and powdery
Alcohol	Moderately high (around 13 %)
Flavors	*Burgundy*: beetroot, raspberries, cassis, cranberries, mulberries, cherries, flowers, spices, herbs, game, earth, tobacco, leather, sandalwood. *Oregon*: Similar to Burgundy *California*: herbs, black cherries, strawberries are common. The better wines have flavors similar to those from Burgundy.
Quality	Burgundy: very good to outstanding Oregon: very good to excellent California: very good to excellent
Locations	Worldwide
Fame	Burgundy France
Longevity	Burgundy: high quality wines in good years can last for two-three decades of more. California: most should be drunk within 6 years; better examples can last a decade of more. Oregon: drink within 6-8 years; better examples can last a decade or more.

Styles	
Côte de Nuits	Rich, suave, concentrated and wonderfully complex. The epitome of Pinot Noir wines.
Côte de Beaune	Less richness and concentration than Côte de Nuits: lighter and less sophisticated.
California	Top examples are similar to Côte de Nuits, but perhaps more forthright. They are generally less complex, less sophisticated, and lack the finesse of high quality French Burgundy.
Oregon	Top examples are similar to Côte de Nuits, but perhaps more forthright. They are generally less complex, less sophisticated and lack the finesse of high quality French Burgundy.

Sangiovese

This varietal produces Italy's most famous wine: Chianti. Two other wines made from this grape, Brunello di Montalcino and Prugnolo Gentle, are less well known, but are generally of higher quality than the run-of-the-mill Chianti. Brunello is unquestionably the superstar of this varietal. It is made from a superior clone of the Sangiovese called Sangiovese Grosso.

Brunello can be big, rich, and complex. At its best, it is one of the finest wines from Italy. Prugnolo Gentle is usually no better than a high quality Chianti, but it is usually more expensive.

Although Chianti is a blended wine, the dominant varietal is Sangiovese. Most Chianti is of poor to average quality; however, a well made wine can be a very special treat: complex, elegant, and very satisfying.

California has limited production of the varietal, but the state is capable of producing some very good wines. Sangiovese Grosso is the dominant clone.

Italy's Super Tuscans can be a single varietal or blend. Sangiovese and Cabernet Sauvignon are frequent grapes in the mix. High quality Super Tuscans can be outstanding: however, many have a shocking price tag.

Profile Sangiovese	
Color	Variable; deep color in the better wines. Early brown tones.
Acids	High
Tannins	Moderate-high
Alcohol	Moderate, high in Brunello
Flavors	Cherries, plums, berries, prunes, herbs, smoke, tar, tobacco, earth, leather, nuts, oak
Quality	Variable; high in a well-made Brunello and in some super Tuscan blends
Locations	Italy, California
Fame	Italy
Longevity	The average wine should be drunk within 4-5 years; better wines can last for a dozen years or more. In great years, Brunello can last for decades.

Syrah

Syrah is grown in many areas around the world, but in the opinion of many, produces its best wines in the northern Rhône Valley of France. The wines of Hermitage and Côte Rôtie represent the supreme varietal expression of this grape. In their youth, the wines are big and tannic; however, as they age, tannins settle down and the wines reveal their startling assemblage of exotic scents and flavors. These can be powerful, full-bodied wines that are slow to mature but long-lived.

Syrah is also a contributor to the blends of the southern Rhône valley; however, Grenache is the dominant grape in most of the blends. Châteauneuf du Pape, Gigondas, Côtes-du-Rhône, and Côtes-du-Ventoux are the most famous wines from the southern Rhône.

Australia produces a more precocious model of the wine. The wines, often called Shiraz in Australia, are riper, softer, and more forward than those of the Rhône Valley, but still deliver a full, rich mouthful of complex, exotic flavors. Tannins are less aggressive, and the fruit is riper, and more dominant, than the wine form the Rhône. Many of the wines are very drinkable on release; however longevity is invariably short. There are, however, many more age worthy wines also produced; Grange Hermitage, Australia's most famous wine, is world-class.

California has been very successful in cultivating wines from this grape. Many are of very good quality, and some are exceptional. The state holds great promise for this varietal and plantings are on the upswing.

Profile Syrah	
Color	Deep
Acids	Moderate to high
Tannins	High
Alcohol	High
Flavors	Raspberries, blackberries, cassis, black cherry, hickory smoke, game, seared meats, black pepper, cloves, cinnamon, tar, grilled nuts, leather, truffles, tobacco, licorice, pine, earth, and minerals
Quality	Very good to exceptional
Locations	Rhône Valley, Australia, California
Fame	Rhône Valley, Australia. However California is gaining in its reputation for producing high quality wines.
Longevity	Rhône Valley: 10-20 year or more California and Australia: 5-10 years

Zinfandel

This grape is almost exclusively grown in California, although its origin has been traced back to Italy (Primitivo), and before that to the Middle East. The wine is made in a variety of styles: white Zinfandel, Rosé, and red styles that range from dry to sweet, and from light to powerful and full-bodied.

Of all the styles, the most successful is the full-bodied red wine crafted similarly to Cabernet Sauvignon. It has a unique, prickly, aggressive mouth feel (described as briery), and is oozing with spicy brambly fruit (blackberries and raspberries). The wine has a panache and verve that is unique. To fully experience the varietal expression of this grape, it should be consumed young. Quality wines have longevity of 6-8 years or more. With age, however, some wines prematurely lose their fruit and become bitter. Acids fall, and the feisty, brambly character of the wine fades.

White Zinfandel, made by pulling the grape skins off the must before color has leached out, is an inexpensive, simple styled wine. However, it has attained great popularity as an every-day drinking wine.

Profile Red Zinfandel	
Color	Variable: deep in the Cabernet style
Acids	Moderate
Tannins	High
Alcohol	High
Flavors	Dominated by blackberries, raspberries, and black pepper; with age develops flavors of cedar, tobacco, chocolate, herbs and spices.
Quality	Very good
Locations	California, Italy (Primitivo)
Fame	California
Longevity	Best to drink within a few years after bottling, but better examples can last for 6-7 years or more. Aging does not improve this varietal. Older wines often become bitter and stale.

WHITE WINES

Chardonnay

Chardonnay is the aristocrat of the white wine grapes. It is grown worldwide and can be made in a variety of styles that range from big, rich, and open to tight, tart, lean and austere.

The most spectacular Chardonnay wines are the white Burgundies, which come from the Burgundy region of France. They reach their summit in the phenomenally rich and powerful wine, Le Montrachet (DRC).

Besides being more subtle and introspective than California Chardonnay, white Burgundies are leaner, tarter, and have less oak, and their flavorful extracts are generally less ripe and forward. They are better wines to pair with foods than the California or Australian renditions.

The wines of Chablis are the leanest, tartest, lightest, and most introspective of all of the white Burgundies, and although they are Chardonnay based, their structure is so disparate that they are in a class by themselves. Most Chablis wines never see oak.

Chardonnay wines from California can be outstanding. The wine critics give most of the accolades to the big, rich, soft tropical fruit flavored wines. Styles similar to the white Burgundies are also produced and can be quite delicious. California and Oregon winemakers oak-age a majority of their wines—sometimes to excess.

Australia's most popular white wine is Chardonnay. They are styled similar to the California model, but are softer, richer, rounder, and fuller. Unfortunately, many lack acidity to the point of being unbalanced. Recently, however, winemakers have been relying on acidification to lighten the weight of their wines and give them a little panache.

New Zealand makes an excellent Chardonnay similar in style to white Burgundy. They have less of the ripe tropical fruity flavors that are so common in the California paradigm. Clean, crisp acidity and more restrained levels of alcohol give the wine a light, delicate, and precise feel. They are versatile wines to serve with a variety of foods.

The Italian rendition is light, tart, and delicately flavored. They lack the richness and body of the California model. However, they are good choices for a variety of moderate to light-bodied foods.

New Zealand is home of some remarkable Chardonnays. They are well-focused, clean, tart, and have less ripe flavors—more like

Burgundy than California. Their lighter weight makes them great accompaniments to a wide variety of foods.

Blanc de Blanc is a style of Champagne that is made entirely from the Chardonnay grape. The still wine (without bubbles) is very tart and relies on the creamy richness of Champagne's mousse (creamy bubbles) to quell the tart harshness of the still wine.

Although the grape is grown worldwide, most other localities have limited success with Chardonnay. However, Chile is making remarkable progress with the varietal, and the grape holds great promise in Spain.

Profile Chardonnay	
Color	Light straw to light golden. Chablis often has a slight green cast.
Acids	*Burgundy*: moderate to high *California*: moderate *Australia*: low to moderate
Alcohol	High
Flavors	Citrus, apples, tropical fruits, pears, melon, butter, toffee, honey, butterscotch, flowers, spices, nuts, figs, smoke, toast, vanilla, earth
Quality	*Burgundy*: very high *Chile:* good to excellent *New Zealand:* good to excellent *California*: good to excellent *Australia*: poor to very good
Locations	Worldwide
Fame	Burgundy, California, Australia, Chile, New Zealand
Longevity	*Burgundy*: typically can last for up to 10 years or more. *California, Chile, New Zealand*: drink within the first 3-4 years. Most will have begun their decline by 4-5 years. *Australia*: drink up on release.

Styles	
California	Rich, ripe, concentrated tropical fruit flavors, varying degrees of oak, moderate acidity. Other styles are leaner and more acidic and have less ripe fruity flavors.
Côte d'Or	Less rich, less oak, less concentrated, more acidic, and more complex than typical California Chardonnay. They are wines of distinction and finesse.
Chablis	Lighter and more introspective than Côte de Beaune, complexity at the expense of concentration. Fruit is less ripe than the typical white Burgundy. Good crisp, clean, acidity; minimal to no oak.
Mâconnais & Chalonnaise (France)	Similar to Côte de Beaune but simpler and less distinctive.
Italy	Very light and tart, delicate flavors, no oak.
New Zealand	Lighter and less ripe than California model; less tropical fruits, no or minimal oak, good crisp acidity.
Australia	Very ripe and full, tropical fruit, oak, low acidity. Richer, bigger, and less acidic than the California rendition. Some are flat and flabby. Recently wines are lighter and have higher levels of acidity.

Chenin Blanc

This grape performs best in the Loire Valley of France where the true varietal character of the grape is expressed. Vouvray, the most popular wine from this varietal, is very high in acidity and needs time to soften before drinking. As it ages in bottle, it often becomes sweeter, as residual sugars that had been hidden under the veil of excessive acidity become exposed.

Another wonderful, steely dry wine from the Loire Valley called Savennières also needs a few years in bottle to allow its tartness to settle down. Unlike most white wines, Savennières and Vouvray are wines that improve with some bottle age.

Coteaux du Layon, Bonnezeaux, and Quarts de Chaume are outstanding sweet wines styled like Sauternes, but lighter, less rich, and not quite as complex. They are medium-full bodied, and have a honey-sweet richness.

Most other Chenin Blanc grapes grown in other parts of the world are of jug wine quality.

Profile Chenin Blanc	
Color	Variable depth- straw to light golden hue
Acids	Loire Valley: very high
Alcohol	Moderate
Flavors	Honey suckle, orange blossoms, apricots, melon, peaches, pears, marzipan, nuts, honey, grass, damp hay
Quality	Loire Valley: Very good—often undervalued Other areas: average
Locations	Loire Valley, California, South Africa, New Zealand
Fame	Loire Valley
Longevity	Loire Valley: some of the elite can last for decades.

Gewürztraminer

This grape produces an unusual wine of exceptional quality. It is grown worldwide, but incontestably makes its best wine in Alsace. There is nothing introspective about Gewürztraminer; the wine lays everything out for you to easily smell and taste.

The flavors are extremely exotic: cold cream, fried bacon, rose petals, ginger, and lichee—what a hodgepodge. The flavors seem discordant, but somehow they magically fit together to produce one of the most unusual wines of the world.

Gewürztraminer has low acidity and high alcohol. If acidity is too low, the wine takes on a cloying oily consistency. In spite of its low acidity, the wine is loaded with flavors and has a remarkable resistance to becoming flabby. However, unduly warm growing seasons usually result in unbalanced, acid-deficient, and cloyingly rich wines. Some wines are sweet; others are bone dry. Flavors are well focused and concentrated, and the wine is gifted with a long and lingering finish.

These are obsequious wines; indeed, their single greatest fault is that they are too obvious: they leave very little to the imagination. However, this shortcoming is overshadowed by the splash of its exotic and phenomenally complex flavor profile. Of all the white wines, most people will agree that Gewürztraminer is the most exotic.

Compared to Alsatian Gewürztraminer, the German version lacks concentration and complexity, and the California rendition is a mere shadow of the Alsatian model. Both are usually sweet, and lack the full spectrum of the grape's varietal character. Of the two, the German rendition is superior. The grape is grown less successfully in many other parts of the world.

Profile Gewürztraminer	
Color	Light golden to deep salmon-copper hue
Acids	Low in Alsace, higher in Germany and California
Alcohol	High in Alsace
Flavors	Lychee, rose petals, cold cream, apricots, tropical fruit, grapefruit, fried bacon, cinnamon, allspice, ginger
Quality	High in Alsace; lower in California and Germany
Locations	Worldwide
Fame	Alsace
Longevity	Drink the average wine in 3-5 years; high quality wines can last for a decade or more.

Pinot Gris

The styles of this wine vary from the light, dry, crisp, and sometimes flavor deficient renditions from Italy, called Pinot Grigio, to the big, rich, soft, and flavorful wines from Alsace known as Tokay d'Alsace. Both dry and sweet versions are produced.

The Alsatian rendition is full-bodied and gifted with a rich complement of exotic flavorful extracts. An orange flavor can be found in many of the wines that can be useful as a marker for the varietal in blind tastings. No other country can consistently match the quality of Alsatian Pinot Gris.

In Germany the grape is known as the Ruländer. While Germany has the ability to make fine examples of the varietal, they are usually weaker, less rich, and do not have the refinement of those from Alsace.

In the United States, Oregon produces very good quality Pinot Gris that, in the best examples, approaches the quality of the Alsatian wine. Most are medium-bodied dry wines that have modest concentrations of flavorful extracts.

The Italian version is tarter and lighter than those made in most other countries. Some are weak and wishy-washy, while others can be excellent. When properly vinified, this can be one of the better white wines produced in Italy

Pinot Gris is an undervalued grape that can make surprisingly high quality wines. They are similar to Chardonnay is style, but their flavorful profile is refreshingly different. Like Chardonnay, acidity is sometimes on the low side.

Profile Pinot Gris	
Color	Spans a spectrum from rich golden-light pink in Alsace to light straw color in Italy.
Acids	Moderate (high in Pinot Grigio)
Alcohol	*Alsace*: high *Oregon*: moderate-high *Germany*: moderate-high *Italy* moderate
Flavors	Oranges, Cointreau, tropical fruits, apricots, apples, lemons, melon, smoke, butter, nuts, butterscotch, and exotic spices
Quality	*Alsace*: very good *Oregon*: average to very good *Germany*: good *Italy*: average to very good
Locations	Alsace, Oregon, Germany, Italy
Fame	Alsace
Longevity	Most should be consumed before 4-5 years of age—the higher quality wines can last for a decade of more.

Riesling

This prestigious grape variety makes one of the world's most famous wines. The grape's solid core of crisp, refreshing acidity supports a complex array of delicate fruity scents and flavors. The premier examples come from Germany and Alsace. The styles of wines from these two countries are diametrically opposite. German wines are light-bodied, sweet, and low in alcohol, while the Alsatian wines are rich, full-bodied, completely dry, and high in alcohol.

There are two main subdivisions of German Rieslings: Mosel-Saar-Ruwer (M-S-R) and Rhine Rieslings. M-S-R wines are light, crisp, delicate, and fresh and are structured with great precision and finesse. Alcohol levels are low, sometimes as low as 7-8%.

Most Rhine wines are not made from the Riesling grape and are of less quality. They are fuller, richer, more substantive, but less crisp than M-S-R wines. Rhine Rieslings focus more on concentration and richness and less on precision and finesse.

Although Riesling is grown worldwide, in locations other than Germany and Alsace, the grape makes good, but seldom great wines. California wines have richness and concentration, but lack the refinement, crispness, and finesse of the German rendition. The painstaking precision of the German and Alsatian model is missing.

The dessert styled wines made from the Riesling grape can be outstanding. Both California and Australia make very fine dessert wines called late harvest Rieslings. Canada also makes a superb Riesling icewine that rivals that of the German rendition. Nevertheless, the best Riesling dessert wines come from Germany.

Profile Riesling	
Color	*Germany*: M-S-R- very light straw colored Rhine- light golden *California*: light golden *Alsace*: light golden
Acids	High
Alcohol	Low
Flavors	Flowers, honey, peaches, apples, quince, orange, passion fruit, citrus, apricots, mango, minerals, and spice
Sugars	*Germany*: dry to very sweet *Alsace*: dry *California*: sweet to very sweet
Quality	*Germany*: high *Alsace*: high *Australia*: good to very good (especially the late harvest wines) *California*: average—late harvest wines can be very good.
Locations	Worldwide
Fame	Germany, Alsace, Canada
Longevity	Variable, quality wines can last for a decade or longer.

Sauvignon Blanc

This outstanding grape is grown worldwide and makes a distinctive wine with unusual aromatic flavors. The most remarkable part of its flavor profile is a distinctive green vegetal, herbal, gooseberry component that, if too pronounced, is uncomplimentary to the wine. However, these unusual flavors are the core of the wine, and if tempered, give it an exotic flare and make it one of the best wines to pair with foods.

The uncomplimentary expressions often applied to this wine, such as weedy, green vegetables, cat's pee, and tomcat's scent would make one think that this wine is the antithesis of savoriness. However, when you taste the wine, you will find it sapid, savory, and a delight to the senses. Blackcurrants, a red-wine flavor uncommon in white wines, is a characteristic flavor in Sauvignon Blanc. This flavor along with its green vegetal component serve as good memory triggers for recognizing this wine in blind tastings.

Sauvignon Blanc is a medium-bodied wine with a good concentration of sapid flavors supported by a solid core of crisp, racy acidity. In some wines you will find a little sweetness due to residual sugars.

In California, a sizable percentage of Sauvignon Blanc wines are oaked and blended with smaller amounts of Sémillon, a soft, rich, and bland varietal. These ministrations make the blend richer in body, more complex, and less acidic, but take away some from its food-friendly nature.

Sauvignon Blanc based white Bordeaux wines are routinely blended with Sémillon plus a smattering of other varietals. Although these can be very good wines, they do not have the quality or the stature of the great red wines of Bordeaux.

The wines of Sancerre and Pouilly Fumé from the Loire Valley of France and the Sauvignon Blanc wines from New Zealand are unblended and unoaked and represent the most unadulterated forms of the varietal. New Zealand has make great strides with this varietal and is producing excellent wines with its own unique flavor profile. Chile also makes good quality Sauvignon Blanc; many are unblended and never see oak.

Good quality dessert wines are also made from this varietal.

Sauvignon Blanc	
Color	Light straw
Acids	High
Alcohol	Averages about 13 %
Flavors	Grass, weeds, herbs, citrus, figs, melon, blackcurrant, gooseberry, apple, nut, unripe fruit, green vegetables, flowers, flint, cat's pee, smoke, minerals, and earth
Quality	Very good
Locations	Worldwide
Fame	Loire Valley, Bordeaux, California, New Zealand
Longevity	Short - Drink within 3 years of bottling.

Styles	
California	Concentrated, oak aged, good acidity, moderate weight Many are blended with Sémillon
Bordeaux	Lighter, less concentrated, more complex than the California model, varying amounts of Sémillon, good acidity, less oak then the California rendition
Loire	No oak, no blending, true varietal character expressed, grassy and smoky flavors, crisp, clean, refreshing acidity, less vegetal flavors than the California model.
New Zealand	No oak, no blending, crisp acidity, true varietal character expressed, fewer grassy, smoky, and vegetal notes, more gooseberry flavor, than the California model.

Sémillon

This grape makes its greatest wines in the Sauternes district of France. In other locations, the grape's lack of acidity and its somewhat stodgy, waxy, lanolin flavors prevent it from becoming a successful pure varietal wine. Australia is one of the few places that produce good quality unblended dry Sémillon wines.

The most famous location of the grape is in the Sauternes district of France. Here, the grape's extracts become concentrated after the berry becomes infected with the noble mold, ***Botrytis Cinerea*** (see German wines). The process, called **noble rot**, makes the grape lose water, thereby concentrating the sugars, acids, and flavorful extracts within the berry.

In the Sauternes district, this grape is blended with Sauvignon Blanc to increase its tartness. Additionally, a dash of Muscadelle is added to the blend to give it additional perfume.

Sauternes are rich, full-bodied, and complex dessert wines of incredible finesse. They are generally regarded as the most elaborate and sophisticated sweet wines of the world.

Profile Sémillon	
Color	Light to moderate golden (deep golden in aged dessert wines)
Acids	Low
Alcohol	High
Flavors	Wax, lanolin, citrus, tangerine, apricot, pineapple, peach, melon, honey, caramel, crème brûlée
Quality	*Australia*: good dry wines and very good dessert wines *California*: very good dessert wines *France*: Sauternes are the most sophisticated and elaborate of dessert wines.
Locations	Worldwide
Fame	Sauternes district of France, Australia
Longevity	Sauternes can last for decades.

Viognier

This grape makes one of the most unique and alluring white wines in France. It reaches its summit in the wines of Château Grillet and Condrieu from the northern Rhône Valley where the grape's varietal character is most accurately expressed.

This is an enchanting wine that has the contrasting qualities of strength and delicacy. It has a big, rich, full-body, yet its low acidity and delicate flavors give it a definite feminine flare. The flavors do not jump out and grab you; rather, you are seduced by their subtlety and charm.

California has numerous plantings of the varietal. Some can be surprisingly good.

Profile Viognier	
Color	Moderate to deep golden color
Acids	Low
Alcohol	High
Flavors	Apricot, peaches, honeydew melon, tropical fruit, pears, lichee, honey suckle, lime blossom, spice
Quality	High
Locations	Northern Rhône Valley, California
Fame	Northern Rhône Valley
Longevity	Drink within 3-4 years

Quiz

Here is a quiz to test your retentive powers. It is important to have a general idea about the more common varietals so that we can work with them in the "matching wine with food" section of this book. True or False:

1. Flavors of blackcurrant (cassis), cedar, and spices are common in Cabernet Sauvignon.

2. Viognier, Sémillon, and Gewürztraminer are low acid wines.

3. Typically, white Burgundy is lighter, tarter, and more introspective than California Chardonnay.

4. "Green flavors" are common in Sauvignon Blanc.

5. M-S-R wines are light-bodied, fruity, and have low levels of alcohol.

6. Sauternes are made from grapes affected with Botrytis Cinerea.

7. Sauternes are typically rich, full-bodied, dry wines.

8. Chenin Blanc produces its best wine in the Loire Valley.

9. Gewürztraminer is a low acid wine with flavors of rose petals, lychee nuts, cold cream, and apricots.

10. Cabernet Sauvignon is a rich, full-bodied wine low in tannins and acids.

11. The typical soft, round California Chardonnay has moderated acidity and tropical fruit flavors.

12. Cabernet Sauvignon has greater acidity and higher tannin levels than Pinot Noir.

13. Mature Pinot Noir is a lush, soft, supple wine with controlled levels of acids and tannins. Dominant flavors include beetroot, cassis, cherries, and exotic spices.

14. Merlot is a soft, supple wine with judicious levels of acids and tannins.

15. Gamay, the grape in Beaujolais, produces wines dominated by fruity flavors and solid levels of acidity. Beaujolais has a relatively short longevity.

16. Acids and tannins progressively decrease as a wine ages.

17. Nebbiolo is the grape that makes the great wines of the Rhône Valley.

18. Syrah is a rich, full-bodied wine with good levels of acids and tannins.

19. Châteauneuf du Pape has some Syrah in its blend.

20. Wines from the Nebbiolo grape have less tannin than wines made from the Gamay grape.

21. Riesling wines from Alsace are high in both acids and alcohol.

22. Riesling wines from Alsace are full-bodied and dry.

23. Viognier is a full-bodied wine low in acids and high in alcohol.

24. Beaujolais is a short-lived, lighthearted wine oozing with fresh, ripe, fruity flavors.

25. Nebbiolo is the dominant grape in the blend of Chianti.

26. The lightest, tartest, and most austere French wine (other than Champagne) made from the Chardonnay grape is Chablis.

27. Mature Pinot Noir is soft, rich, round and complex.

28. The greatest wines made from the Pinot Noir grape are the red Burgundies.

29. Black pepper, raspberries, and blackberries are common scents in Zinfandels.

30. Chardonnay wines from Australia are typically low in acidity and abound with rich tropical fruit.

31. The Gamay grape makes wines that are short lived but rich in fruity flavors.

32. Chardonnay is typically heavier and less tart than Sauvignon Blanc.

33. Zinfandel should be consumed when young to preserve its fresh, aggressive character.

34. Green flavors are common in Chardonnay wines.

35. Chablis is one of the lightest wines made from the Chardonnay grape.

Answers

All answers are true except for #7, 10, 17, 20, 25, and 34.

CHAPTER 7
Regional Characteristics

This chapter will give you a short summary of some of the more important wine growing regions around the world. It is not meant to be thoroughly descriptive, but will give you a general idea of how the styles and varietal characteristics change when the same grape is grown in different climates and soils and molded by a winemaker who may have a different philosophy about how the varietal should be fashioned. Full descriptions of the characteristics of many of the wines discussed are not given in this chapter, but the essential nature of these wines can be found in the previous chapter on "Varietals."

This chapter is a great reference. Before you go to a wine tasting, look up the wine's characteristics so that you will know what to look for when you smell and sip. Reading about wines is important, but there is nothing better than tasting a wine and discussing it with your friends. In so doing, you will be more successful in remembering the salient features of the wine. Keep in mind that the descriptions below are for typical wines, and there may be significant departures in their portrayal that are related to effects produced by weather, disease, wine making techniques and an array of other factors.

THE MYSTIQUE OF THE WINE LABEL

Across the world, wines are named in a hodgepodge fashion. This mishmash of wine labeling is exceedingly confusing to the novice as well as the wine aficionado. In Italy, for example, some wines are named after the town from which they are made such as *Orvieto*; others are named after the grape varietal, such as Barbara. Still others have weird exotic names such as *Lacrima Christi,* which means "tears of Christ." Wines made from the same varietals can have totally different labels. There are so many different wine names in Italy that it is next to impossible to remember them all.

French wines are a little more logical. Most are named after locations. Bordeaux wines have the word Châteaux affixed to their name. The word Châteaux, which means house, is used for estates that have a vineyard attached and is an indication that the wine is from Bordeaux. Unfortunately, Bordeaux wines are composed of variable blends of a composite of several different grapes; the predominant ones being Cabernet Sauvignon, Merlot, and Cabernet Franc.

Although Burgundy wines are also named after a location, several different wine makers may own a particular vineyard plot. For example, *Clos de Vougeot* is a vineyard parcel subdivided into over five-dozen different plots. All plots will have Clos de Vougeot printed on the label, however, different producers own each plot. In essence, the property produces over five-dozen different wines. The name of the producer is therefore of paramount importance when you purchase Burgundy wines.

New World wines have a much more logical labeling system. Most wines are named after the grape varietal and the company that produced them. A California wine labeled Robert Mondavi Cabernet Sauvignon was made by the Robert Mondavi wine company and the predominant grape in the blend is Cabernet Sauvignon. In the United States, a wine named after a particular varietal must contain at least 75% of that varietal; the rest of the blend is anybodies guess. This system of labeling is also found in other wine producing states in the United States such as Washington and Oregon.

The terms Private Reserve or Special Selection on the California label usually indicate a wine of higher quality than the regular bottling; however, the terms are not regulated and the use of the term is up to the discretion of the winemaker. Sometimes, the regular bottling is of equal quality to those designated Private Reserve or Special Selection, but the price will be significantly higher. In an attempt to sell their wines, some unscrupulous wine producers will label all of their production as Private Reserve. Nevertheless, quality producers, such as Caymus and Robert Mondavi, will reserve the term for wines that are a cut above the regular bottling.

Labels from Australia are even more informative than in California. If the wine contains more than one varietal, it will name the predominant varietal first and the secondary blending grape second and so forth. For example consider the wine Penfolds Cabernet Shiraz. The company that produced the wine is Penfolds and the blend is predominantly Cabernet Sauvignon with lesser amounts of Shiraz.

Sometimes Australian wines may only use initials of the varietals: Penfold's G-S-M stands for Grenache, Shiraz, and Mouvedre.

AUSTRALIA

There is no doubt that the superstar of Australia's wine industry is Shiraz. However, there are many other noteworthy varietals grown in this country. Cabernet Sauvignon and Chardonnay are very successful varietals that have a strong foothold in the industry. The Aussies also produce an impressive array of high quality dessert wines. Quality in Australian wines has been constantly improving, and many of the wines are extremely good values.

Shiraz: Although the spelling is a little different, this is the same grape as the Syrah from the Rhône Valley of France. Some producers in Australia also use the spelling Syrah. When properly vinified, Shiraz can be outstanding. These are full-bodied wines with moderate to high alcohol levels. Flavorful extracts are maintained by a generous infusion of fruit supporting acidity. The wines are less aggressive and are approachable sooner than Syrah from the Rhône Valley. This is due to lower levels of tannins and the ripe nature of the fruity extracts. The flavor profile is typical for the Syrah grape.

Cabernet Sauvignon: The fruity flavors are riper, and the acids are lower than those of the California rendition; however, the wine has good levels of firm tannins. Because of the low levels of acidity, these wines are supple, soft, and round. Some can be quite luscious. If skillfully vinified, high quality wines can be produced.

Cabernet/Shiraz blends can be outstanding. Shiraz tempers the harsher tannins of Cabernet, while at the same time bolsters Cabernet's low acidity.

Pinot Noir**:** The typical wine lacks complexity and refinement. Most are no better than average quality. Nevertheless, there are occasional wines of very good quality produced. Tasmania holds great promise for the Pinot Noir varietal.

Chardonnay**:** These wines are rich and full-bodied, but fruit-supporting acidity is often deficient. Tropical fruit flavors abound. Oak aging further softens and adds weight and richness to these already hefty wines. Successful wines are soft, rich, and lush, but longevity is often short. Because of their weight and low levels of acidity, they have limited use in wine-food pairings.

In recent vintages, many of the winemakers have increased acidity levels, most usually by the addition of tartaric acid, which has resulted in crisper, lighter styled wines. Fat and flabby renditions are becoming increasingly less common.

Sauvignon Blanc: Although the wine has good levels of acidity, the low levels of flavorful extract and excesses in green flavors mar the character of this wine. Quality is no better than average.

Sémillon: This is a successful grape variety in Australia. Wine makers produce both sweet and dry unblended wines. The sweet versions are made from grapes affected with *Botrytis Cinerea* and are crafted in a style similar to Sauternes. Quality can be very high. Dry styles can also be quite good. Adequate levels of acidy support an array of typical varietal flavors. The dry Australian rendition is crisper, and more spirited than those produced in California.

Riesling: The Aussies call this grape the Rhine Riesling. Good to excellent wines are regularly produced. Although they do not match the quality of the German rendition, they are sound wines with good varietal character. Some of the dessert wines can be outstanding.

Muscat (Muscat of Alexandria): These are very sweet wines of exceptionally high quality that have excellent aging potential. The wines are full-bodied and have very concentrated and complex flavorful extracts. Look for flavors of grapes, roses, caramel, crème brûlée, spices, butter, honey, nuts, apricots, oranges, and melon.

Tawny Port: Although constructed quite differently from the classic wine from Portugal, the wine is remarkably good and very inexpensive.

CHILE

Chile has the potential of producing very high quality wines. The soil and climate are ideal; however, the industry has suffered from lack of funding and has been hampered by outdated equipment and inferior vinification techniques. Nonetheless, over the past few years, several prestigious foreign investors have supplied funding and know-how, and the quality of the wines have significantly improved—some are very impressive. Most of Chile's vineyards occupy the Central Valley, which lies between the costal range and the Andes. For the most part, the wines are marketed with varietal labeling. The most successful varietals are Cabernet Sauvignon, Merlot, Syrah, Chardonnay, Sauvignon Blanc and Carmenere. Like in many places worldwide, they are struggling with Pinot Noir.

The following is a description of the more popular varietals.

Chardonnay: Most have good levels of fruit supporting acidity, prudent amounts of oak, and less of the rich, ripe tropical fruity flavors that are so common in the California rendition. Some are of very high quality and represent very good values.

Sauvignon Blanc: The wines are crisp, clean, lively and refreshing. They have less of the herbal, green vegetal flavors and more citrus and gooseberry flavors. Many of the wine are not oaked or blended and are similar in structure and flavor to the New Zealand model.

Cabernet Sauvignon: This is a rich, round, wine with soft powdery tannins and well-focused varietal flavors. As the growing season is long, the tannins have a chance to ripen on the vine making many of the wines ready to drink soon after bottling. The more prestigious renditions are age worthy and need time in bottle; many are of very high quality.

Merlot: The charming, silky and supple Merlots from this country can stack up to the very best. They are incredibly rich, soft, and flavorful. The flavor profile is typical for the varietal.

Syrah: The long ripening season in Chile allows much of the tannins to ripen on the vine, rather than in the bottle. The wine is rich, fruity, concentrated and complex. What little the wine may lack in sophistication, it more than compensates for by the sheer magnitude of its richness and strength.

Carmenere: This varietal has a broodingly dark color and an array of concentrated and complex flavors. Look for flavors of berries, plums, soy, roasted peppers, black tea, and chocolate. Quality wines have a rich, concentrated and amazingly complex aftertaste. Carmenere is exclusively a Chilean wine and the bargain of their industry. These wines have a short longevity and should be consumed soon after bottling.

FRANCE

France is a vast wine-producing region that creates wines in a parade of different styles. The portraits given for the wines below are for typical wines from each region. Deviation from the classical models can change from year to year and from place to place.

Alsace

The grape varieties in this region are similar to those in Germany: Riesling, Pinot Gris, Pinot Blanc, Muscat, and Gewürztraminer. They differ from the German renditions in that they are higher in alcohol, richer and fuller, and the majority is made totally dry. The unusual scents and flavors of roses and oranges are found in many Alsatian wines.

- Riesling: This is a totally dry wine, high in alcohol and full-bodied. It has a full complement of rich, fresh, varietal flavors that are bolstered by clean, crisp, acidity. The Alsatians consider this their premier wine.

- **Pinot Gris**: Known locally as Tokay d'Alsace, this wine is rich and full-bodied, but typically has low levels of acidity. It is Chardonnay-like in structure. Pinot Gris is made in both dry and sweet styles. The Alsatian rendition represents the best varietal expression of the grape.

- **Pinot Blanc**: This varietal makes wine similar to Chardonnay in style and taste; however, the wines are on a lesser plateau of quality. Compared to Chardonnay, they are less complex and usually have lower concentrations of fruity flavors; nevertheless, they represent some of the best renditions of this varietal.

- **Muscat**: Worldwide, the great majority of these wines are made in a rich and sweet style. However, in Alsace, they are light-bodied and bone dry. The wine is aromatic and has delicate flavors of musk, grapes, tropical fruits, melons, and flowers—especially roses. Longevity is short. Drink these wines within their first few years of life.

- **Gewürztraminer:** Without doubt, the best varietal expression of this grape comes from Alsace. It is a rich, full-bodied, obsequious wine with a full bevy of concentrated and easily appreciated exotic scents and flavors. The concentration of alcohol is high and acidity is low, which gives the wine a thick and sometimes oily feel on the palate. However, in spite of this precarious construction, the wine has a remarkable resistance to becoming flabby. Gewürztraminer is made in both sweet and dry styles.

There is often sweetness in the wine—even in those not designated as sweet. Wines labeled *Vendange Tardive* are medium sweet. The dessert style, called *Selection des Grains Nobles*, is scrumptious.

Bordeaux

Vin, Monsieur Maurois?

Some of the greatest wines in the world come from this relatively small area in France. Bordeaux is composed of four major wine producing districts: Médoc, Graves (including Sauternes), Pomerol, and St-Emilion. The Médoc is further subdivided into Saint Estèphe, Pauillac, Saint Julien, Margaux and a few other less prestigious districts.

It is often difficult to distinguish a well-made Bordeaux wine from a California Cabernet Sauvignon or Meritage. However, Bordeaux wines are usually less dense in color and are more introspective than their California cousins. There is no arguing that they have a greater longevity. Descriptions below are for typical wines from the region.

Médoc

The wines from the Médoc are the quintessential examples of the Bordeaux model, yet the various districts of the Médoc have subtle differences of their own.

Saint Estèphe: These are powerful wines that are full-bodied and high in tannins. They are a blend of Cabernet Sauvignon with lesser amounts of Merlot and token amounts of other varietals. Typically, Saint Estèphe wines have strength at the expense of elegance. However, some of Bordeaux's most sophisticated wines come from this district. The most distinguished producers are Château **Cos d'Estournel** and **Château Montrose.**

Pauillac: These are rich, deeply colored, full-bodied wines that have a strong Cabernet Sauvignon varietal character. They have power and strength, yet they are elegant and refined. The blend is predominantly Cabernet Sauvignon with lesser amounts of Merlot and smatterings of other varietals. These are sophisticated wines of great style and grace. Some of the greatest wines of the world come from this district. The most famous are the three great growths: **Château Lafite Rothschild, Château Mouton Rothschild,** and **Château Latour.** Other notable wines from the region include **Château Pichon-Longueville Comtesse de Lalande, Château Lynch-Bages, Château Grand-Puy-Lacoste, Château Haut-Batailley, and Château Pontet-Canet.**

Saint Julien: The most typical wines of the Médoc come from this district. They are soft, elegant, and sophisticated wines that have a full and complex nose. Cabernet Sauvignon is the dominant varietal with Merlot filling in most of the remainder of the blend. The wines are lighter, softer, suppler, and more elegant than the typical Pauillac rendition. Some of the most famous wines of the region include: **Château Léoville-Las Cases, Château Ducru-Beaucaillou, Château Gruaud-Larose, Château Léoville-Barton, Château Talbot, Château Beychevelle.**

Margaux: The typical wine is similar in structure to those of Saint Julien, but perhaps a bit lighter and less sophisticated. These wines have a great nose—the best of the Médoc wines. The most prestigious wine is the first growth, **Château Margaux.** Other notable wines include **Château Palmer, Château Giscours, Château La Lagune, Château Lascombes, Château Cantemerle** and **Château Boyd-Cantenac.** There are many wines of lesser quality from this district.

Graves

This district produces both red and white wines. The famous white Bordeaux wines, made from a blend of Sauvignon Blanc and Sémillon, are good sound wines, but of lesser quality than the reds. They are similar in structure to California Sauvignon Blanc but more complex and perhaps not quite as rich.

Cabernet Sauvignon is the dominant grape in most of the red blends; however, in some wines Merlot dominates. These wines have a relaxed, loose-knit structure, and well-focused flavors that are easy to perceive. They are lighter in colors and develop brown tones earlier than the Médoc wines. The most famous reds are **Château Haut Brion** and **Château La Mission Haut Brion.**

Pomerol

In this region, Merlot reaches its crescendo and is the dominant grape in the blends. The wines have high concentrations of complex flavorful extracts and a unique, smooth, silky, soft mouth feel. **Château Pétrus** is the superstar of the region, but **Château Trotanoy** is a close runner-up. Other excellent wines from the area include **Château Lafleur, Château L'Evangile, Château La Conseillante, Château Latour à Pomerol,** and **Vieux Château Certan.**

Saint-Émilion

These wines are a blend of Merlot, Cabernet Franc, and lesser amounts of Cabernet Sauvignon. The typical wine is soft, fleshy, and has a mineral, earthy flavor. They are lighter and less rich than the wines from Pomerol. The standout wines are **Château Cheval Blanc** and **Château Ausone.** Other touted wines from the region include **Château Figeac, Château Magdelaine,** and **Château Canon.**

Burgundy

Burgundy is composed of five main regions: Chablis, Côte D'Or, Côte Chalonnaise, Mâconnais, and Beaujolais. All white Burgundies are made exclusively from the Chardonnay grape. Red Burgundies are made from the Pinot Noir grape with the exception of Beaujolais, which is made entirely from Gamay.

Grand Cru wines are of highest quality; *Premier Cru* are, in most cases, a definite step down, and the *village wines* represent the lesser wines of the township. However, there are many discrepancies in this scheme. In some instances a *Premier Cru* may be superior to a *Grand*

Cru. In other instances, *Grand Cru* and *Premier Cru* wines may not be deserving of their ranking.

The labels on Burgundy wines are very confusing. In many instances, the words *Grand Cru* and *Premier Cru* are not printed on the label; however, there are some clues. In *Premier Cru* wines, the village name and the vineyard name are usually printed on the label in the same large print, usually one below the other. In *Grand Cru* wines, only the vineyard name is printed on the label. Village wines are named after the village from which they are made: Gevrey-Chambertin, Aloxe-Corton, Nuits-Saint-Georges, etc. The village of Gevrey attached the name of its most famous vineyard, Chambertin (a *Grand Cru*), to its name. For example, the Grand Cru is called "Chambertin," the village wine is called "Gevrey-Chambertin."

Another confusing aspect of the label is that single vineyards are often divided into parcels, with each parcel being owned by different proprietors. The quality of the wines produced by each proprietor can differ greatly. Therefore, the name of the proprietor is very important when selecting a wine.

Chablis

Chablis is made entirely from the Chardonnay grape. Because of its cold northern climate, the grapes frequently do not fully ripen. This gives the wine a pale straw color that often has a slight green cast. The wine has moderate levels of alcohol and a light to medium weigh. It is high in crisp, refreshing acidity, but flavors are restrained and introspective. The great majority of these wines never see oak. Chablis is considerably lighter, crisper, tarter, and more contemplative than California Chardonnay. The *Grand Cru* wines in good years are spectacular. The *Premier Cru* wines are a definite step down, and those labeled simply as Chablis are often pedestrian. Avoid wines labeled *Petite Chablis*; they are invariably of poor quality.

Côte D'Or

This is the home of some of the most magnificent wines in the world. Indeed, the Pinot Noir grape reaches perfection in this small region. Most connoisseurs consider red Burgundy to be the world's most celebrated wine.

The **Côte D'Or** is geographically divided into the **Côte de Nuits** (southern end) and the **Côte de Beaune** (northern end). The Côte de Beaune is more famous for white wines and the Côte de Nuits for its reds.

Mature quality red Burgundies are rich, soft, elegant wines that have great concentration and complexity. Acids and tannins are restrained. Ripe fruity flavors, low acidity, and solid alcohol levels give the wine a rich, sweet character. The flavor profile for the wine is typical Pinot Noir. The flavor of beetroot is a good marker for the varietal.

The longevity of red Burgundies is considerably shorter than that of red Bordeaux wines. Nonetheless, great wines in outstanding years can last for tens of years, but the average wines should be tried when they are six to seven years old. Although one thinks of red Burgundies as being soft and round, young wine with great longevity will be dark in color and have a good infusion of aggressive acids and tannins.

White Burgundies are a little lighter and more tart and introspective than the typical California Chardonnay. They generally see less oak, which gives them a lighter feel on the palate. Ripe tropical fruit flavors are less common, but the wine retains the typical Chardonnay flavor profile. Great white Burgundies from top years can last for ten years or more. They have greater life expectancy than California Chardonnay, most of which will be in decline three to five years after bottling. Don't be fooled by the golden color of older white Burgundies. If the wine is crystal clear and brilliant, it is probably still sound.

Red Wines from the Côte D'Or

Gevrey-Chambertin (Côte de Nuits): Gevrey-Chambertin is the name of a village that has affixed its most famous vineyard, Chambertin, to its name. The wines have a deep Burgundy color and a big, rich, full-body; yet, in spite of their masculine features, they are soft, smooth, and lavish. Judicious levels of acidity support rich, concentrated, and complex varietal flavors. There are 9 *Grand Crus* and all have Chambertin affixed to their name. Note, however, that wines labeled "Gevrey-Chambertin" are village wines. Some of the famous *Grand Crus* include Chambertin, Chambertin Clos de Bèze, Charmes-Chambertin and Chapelle-Chambertin.

Morey-Saint-Denis (Côte de Nuits): This is a famous red wine region, similar to Gevrey-Chambertin, but a bit lighter and more refined. There are five *Grand Crus*. The most famous are **Bonnes Mares, Clos de La Roach,** and **Clos de Tart.**

Chambolle-Musigny (Côte de Nuits): The wine is lighter colored, less concentrated, and has softer tannins than Gevrey-Chambertin. Its greatest asset is its wonderful complex nose. This is an elegant wine with delicate flavors and a definite feminine flare. There are two famous *Grand Crus*: **Bonnes-Mares** (shared with Morey-Saint-Denis) and **Musigny**.

Vougeot (Côte de Nuits): These wines are similar to Chambolle-Musign, but are not quite as fragrant. Clos de Vougeot is the *Grand Crus*. The vineyard is divided into several dozen parcels, each owned by a different proprietor. As you might expect, under these conditions the character and quality of the wines coming from this site can be quite variable in both style and quality.

Vosne-Romanée (Côte de Nuits): This area represents the crescendo of red Burgundy wine production. The wines are rich, concentrated, complex, and exotic. Some of the greatest red wines in the world come from this region. The famous *Grand Crus* are **Échézeaux, Grands Échézeaux, La Romanée, Romanée St.-Vivant, Richebourg, La Tâche, and Romanée-Conti**. Most connoisseurs consider Romanée-Conti and La Tâche to be the archetypical examples of red Burgundy.

Nuits-Saint-Georges (Côte de Nuits): These are good solid red wines with a rich, full-body and a good complement of concentrated flavorful extracts, but they lack some in sophistication. There are no *Grand Crus*.

Aloxe-Corton (Côte de Beaune): Typically, these wines are unsophisticated and loose-knit. They are medium-bodied and have moderate concentration and complexity. The single exception is the great red wine, **Corton,** a *Grand Crus.* It is the superstar of the region, and most consider it to be the best red wine from the Côte de

Beaune. It can be a wonderful wine: rich, concentrated, and complex; however, in off years it can be quite ordinary.

Beaune (Côte de Beaune): Although this town is the hub of the great Burgundy commerce, its red wines are generally of average quality. These are medium-bodied, soft textured wines with moderate concentration and complexity. There are no *Grand Crus.*

Pommard (Côte de Beaune): The majority of the wines are full, rich, concentrated, and loosely knit. Flavors are well focused and easy to appreciate. In great years, these wines can be marvelous. There are no *Grand Crus.*

Volnay (Côte de Beaune): These are light, loose-textured, feminine styled wines with delicate flavors and an ethereal, highly perfumed nose. There are no *Grand Crus.*

White Wines from the Côte D'Or

Corton Charlemagne (Côte de Beaune): This is the great *Grand Crus* from Aloxe-Corton. These wines are tight in their youth, and take a little time to ripen. When mature, they are rich, complex, full-bodied, and highly concentrated. Their characteristic chalky, nutty, flavor is supported by a good dose of crisp acidity. In good years, these are distinctive wines with great finesse and outstanding quality.

Auxey-Duresses (Côte de Beaune): Similar to Meursault (below), but not as distinguished.

Meursault (Côte de Beaune): The light golden color of these wines is a tip off to their ripeness. They are rich, mellow, and loaded with soft Chardonnay fruity flavors. Acidity is on the low side. Their loose-knit structure and full, savory nose gives them a sybaritic flare. Be careful not to store these wines too long, as most have a short longevity. There are no *Grand Crus.*

Puligny-Montrachet (Côte de Beaune): The *Grand Cru* are the richest and most concentrated of the white Burgundies. Top examples are lush, sumptuous, and of very high quality. The *Premier Cru* are lighter, lower in alcohol, higher in acidity, and a definite step down in stature. The village wines are variable in quality, but still good sound wines. The *Grand Crus* are **Le Montrachet, Chevalier-Montrachet, Bâtard-Montrachet**, and **Bienvenues-Bâtard-Montrachet**. Le Montrachet (DRC) is the quintessence of white Burgundies. Indeed, it can be argued that it is the epitome of all white wines.

Chassagne-Montrachet (Côte de Beaune): Similar to Puligny-Montrachet; however, the village wines are more dependable and a little higher in quality. *Grand Crus*: **Le Montrachet, Bâtard-Montrachet** (both shared with Puligny-Montrachet)

Côte Chalonnaise

This region has five appellations: Bouzeron, Rully, Mercury, Givry, and Montagny. Both red and white wines are produced. Much of the wine is quite average. **Mercury** has the capability of producing good quality white and red wines and is generally considered the best appellation of the region. There are no *Grand Crus.*

Mâconnais

Most of the wines from the region are of ordinary quality. However the appellations of Macon-Villages, St. Véran, and Pouilly-Fuissé have the capacity to produce very good white wines. There are no *Grand Crus.*

Mâcon-Villages: These wines have a village name attached to the appellation such as Mâcon-Chorine or Mâcon Lugny. Some can be quite good: clean, crisp, and elegant; however, most are ordinary.

Saint-Véran Wines from this appellation are consistently of good quality. They are richer, smoother, and fuller than the village wine and are loaded with clean, well-focused Chardonnay fruit.

Pouilly-Fuissé wines have a wide spectrum of quality. The appellation has the ability to make the best wines of the region; however, many disappointing wines are also made. The better wines have good balance and loads of concentrated Chardonnay fruit supported by crisp, refreshing acidity. Lesser wines are weak, flat, and lack concentration.

Beaujolais

The Gamay grape produces the wonderful, lively, crisp, fruity wines of Beaujolais. These are not sophisticated wines; however, they are bright, lively, exceedingly drinkable, and pleasure provoking wines.

Beaujolais wines are medium-red in color and loaded with rousing, fresh fruity flavors. They have a solid core of refreshing acidity, a medium body, and relatively low levels of tannins. The wine should be drunk young and slightly chilled.

The best wines come from ten superior villages called crus Beaujolais: **Brouilly, Côte de Brouilly, Régnié, Morgon, Chiroubles, Fleurie, Moulin-a-Vent, Chénas, Juliénas, and Saint-Amour.** The crus wines will have the name of the village prominently displayed on the label, The word "Beaujolais" is often in small print at the bottom of the label.

Champagne

C'est très bien!

The stature of Champagne depends on both the quality of the still wine and the character of the bubbles. The mouth-feel of Champagne is a paramount consideration in regard to quality, and is intricately tied to the character of the bubbles.

THE STILL WINE

Grapes for the highest quality Champagnes are grown in chalky soil around the French cities of Reims and Epernay. Champagne is made from three different grapes. The two red grapes are Pinot Noir and Pinot Meunier; the white grape is Chardonnay.

Champagne made from the red grapes is called ***Blanc de Noirs***. These wines have a faint tint of salmon to their color and are richer and more flavorful than Chardonnay based wines. In the production of these wines, the skin is pulled from the must before color and tannins leach out. Flavors in Blanc de Noirs Champagnes include apples, cherries, strawberries, berries, citrus, tropical fruit, and nuts. Note the interesting mixture of red and white fruit flavors.

Champagnes made from Chardonnay are called ***Blanc de Blancs***. They are light, elegant, and more introspective than the Blanc de Noirs. Flavors include apples, citrus, earth, nuts, bread dough, yeast, butter, butterscotch, coconut, spice, smoke, and ginger. Blanc de Blancs are less common than Blanc de Noirs.

Most Champagne is a blend of both red and white grapes. To keep consistency in quality and flavor, current vintages are blended with prior vintages. Vintage dates will not be found on these bottles.

In outstanding years the winemaker may choose not to blend his wine with prior years. These wines will receive a vintage date and are bottled as **Vintage Champagne.**

THE BUBBLES

Acidity in the still wine of Champagne is harsh and unpleasant. It is the soft, round feel of Champagne's tiny, creamy bubbles that assuages the aggressive tartness of the still wine. Lesser quality Champagnes lack a creamy mousse and consequently will have a rough and tart feel on the palate. Large coarse bubbles that explode on contact with the mouth (like soda pop) will accentuate the harshness of the still wine with their nettlesome attack.

High quality Champagne will have a mousse composed of tiny, evenly spaced, uniform sized pinpoint carbonation that imparts a soft, creamy feeling to the mouth. This creamy foam is what gives Champagne its festive nature.

It is the dichotomy in the duality of creaminess and tartness that makes Champagne such a great wine to serve with so large a diversity of foods. A round, soft, creamy mouth feel is not found in tart table wines; rather, the aggressive angularity of their acidity is the antithesis of round creaminess. Champagne has the best of both worlds—tartness plus roundness. As you read on in future chapters, you will see how the integration of creamy roundness and crisp acidity gives Champagne such a wide range of versatility in regard to wine-food pairings.

The quality of Champagne is dependent upon a unique process called **Méthode Champenoise**, which is the traditional French method of making Champagne by fermenting wine in bottle. Other methods of production invariably lead to lower quality Champagnes.

Dry Champagne is called **Brut; Extra Dry** has a bit more sweetness, and then in increasing degrees of sweetness there is **Sec, Demi-Sec, and Doux.** Wines labeled **Crémant** are under a little less pressure, and the mousse is generated with a little less gusto.

Rosé Champagne is made by leaving the red grape skins in contact with the must for a little longer period of time or by blending in a little red wine. The wines are richer and frequently have a pronounced strawberry flavor. They can be quite delicious; however, some brands can be very expensive. This is especially true for French Rosé Champagne.

The better producers include the following: **Bollinger, Heidsieck Monopole, Krug, Moët & Chandon, Mug, Perrier-Jouët, Louis Roederer, Taittinger, Ruinart, Veuve Cliquot, Piper Heidsieck, Charles Heidsieck,** and **Pommery.**

Loire Valley

The Loire Valley is located in northern France where weather is less than ideal for grape ripening. However, in clement years, high quality wines are regularly produced.

Pouilly-Fumé: This is one of the most famous wines from the Loire Valley. The wine is made from pure, unblended Sauvignon Blanc. The color is pale straw often with a faint green tinge. These are medium bodied wines that have a good solid core of clean, crisp acidity. Flavors are typical for the varietal, but there are less of the vegetal flavors so common in the California model. These wines are unblended, never see oak, and represent one of the unadulterated versions of this varietal. Although they have good acidity, they have a short longevity. Drink within 3 years.

Sancerre: These are lighter, tarter, and not quite as rich as Pouilly-Fumé, but they are made in the same fashion and from the same grape variety. Their general characteristics and flavors are similar to Pouilly-Fumé; however, production is higher, and the wines are more readily available.

Vouvray: This wine is made from the Chenin Blanc grape in and around the famous French province of Touraine. Acidity is very high and often masks residual sugars, which emerge as acid levels fall. The wines are packed with concentrated and complex flavors of apples, honey, herbs, pineapple, citrus, spices, and nuts. Give these wines time in bottle to settle down. Sweet versions can last decades; the dry rendition should be consumed within 5-6 years.

Chinon: Chinon is a little town in the province of Touraine. The wine, made from the Cabernet Franc grape, is dry and light to medium weight. In good years, the wine is fresh, fruity, fragrant, and alluring. Look for raspberries, blackberries, strawberries, plums, blackcurrant, violets, coffee, olives, smoke, herbs, meat, licorice, and minerals. Top vintages can last for 8-10 years. Lesser vintages are thin and tart—drink these soon after bottling.

Bourgueil: This is a light-bodied, delicate, and charming wine made from Cabernet Sauvignon and Cabernet Franc. Tannins are low and good crisp levels of acidity support bright fruity flavors.

Savennières: These are unblended wines made from the Chenin Blanc grape. Very high levels of acidity demand that the wines age for a few years prior to drinking. When mature, they become rich, concentrated, and complex. Look for apples, citrus, peaches, lime, flowers, herbs, minerals, and almonds. Some of these wines can age for ten years or more.

Muscadet: The wine has the same name as the grape. These are very dry, subtle, fruity, light-bodied wines that are high in acidity. Flavors are delicate and fleeting. Drink these wines within two or three years of bottling.

Coteaux du Layon: Very sweet dessert wines with sound acidity are made in this small region of France. They are produced from wizened Chenin Blanc grapes that have been attacked by the noble mold, *Botrytis cinerea* (see German wines). **Bonnezeaux** and **Quarts**

de Chaume are two famous crus from this appellation. The wines are lighter, tarter and not as sophisticated as a top quality Sauternes. Solid levels of acidity support flavors of oranges, orange blossoms, pineapples, peaches, apricots, raisins, honey, and crème brûlée.

Rhône Valley

Oui, Châteauneuf-du-Pape, s'il vous plaît

The valley is divided into northern and southern parts. In the north, Syrah is the premier red wine grape, whereas in the south, the wines are blends of Grenache, Syrah, Mourvèdre, Cinsaut and scatterings of a montage of other varietals.

Rhône white wines made from Viognier, Roussanne, and Marsanne grapes are rich and full-bodied. Roussanne and Marsanne blends make wines similar in style to Chardonnay; however, they are perhaps a little bigger, and have higher levels of acidity.

Northern Rhône

Côte Rôtie: This is an outstanding red wine that typically takes several years to mature. In their youth they are tart and tannic.

However, at maturity, these are refined wines packed with Syrah varietal flavors. Top vintages can age for 25 years or more. Quality is very high.

Château Grillet and Condrieu: These two famous white wine appellations produce wines entirely from the Viognier grape. It is in this region that the Viognier grape reaches its crescendo. The wines are golden in color and have a soft, rich mouth feel. They are full-bodied, yet the flavors are very delicate and introspective. Drink within their first four years. Wines from top vintages are outstanding. In poor years, the wines are flat and flavorless.

St.-Joseph: The red wines are softer, lighter, and riper than Côte Rôtie, and have lower levels of acids and tannins. Nevertheless, they still deliver a big mouthful of Syrah varietal flavors. Quality can be high; however, the wines lack the elegance, finesse, concentration, and sophistication of Côte Rôtie. Big, rich, full-bodied white wines made from Roussanne and Marsanne grapes are also produced.

Crozes Hermitage: Although coarser and generally of lower quality then St.-Joseph, these wines are richer and more concentrated. In top years, high quality wines are produced. Very good quality white wines from Roussanne and Marsanne grapes are also produced.

Hermitage: About seventy percent of the wine produced in this locality is red. Although equal in quality to *Côte Rôtie,* Hermitage is more refined, precise, and has a little less weight. It is a deeply colored, concentrated wine that can be rather aggressive in its youth. Tannins are high and acidity can be assertive. It takes several years for the wine to soften enough to expose the myriad of complex flavors buried within.

White wines made from a blend of Roussanne and Marsanne grapes are full-bodied, rich, ripe, and fleshy. Solid levels of acidity support an assembly of concentrated and complex scents and flavors. Look for savors of flowers, peaches, apples, pears, tropical fruits, figs, grilled nuts, dried fruits, honey, mint, toffee, and licorice. Quality wines can last for decades! White Hermitage is one of the longest-lived white wines.

Cornas: These inky black-purple wines are tannic monsters that take 8-10 years to shed their tannins; however, at maturity, they are robust, full-bodied and loaded with rich, concentrated flavors. The sediment formed in these wines can be prodigious. Although Cornas can be of very good quality, it lacks the precision and sophistication of Hermitage.

Southern Rhône

Gigondas: The blend of this wine is predominantly Grenache with lesser amounts of Syrah, Mourvèdre and dashes of other varietals. Gigondas is a very full-bodied wine with alcohol content often in excess of 14%. Look for flavors of raspberries, cassis, cherries, black pepper, coffee, tobacco, chocolate, and leather. Although these wines are approachable at a young age, good quality wines can age for 10 years or more.

Châteauneuf-du-Pape: This is the most prestigious wine from southern Rhône. It is a blend of 13 varietals. The dominant grape varietal is Grenache; lesser amounts of Syrah, Mourvèdre, Cinsault and scatterings of others fill out the remainder of the blend. This is a rich, full-bodied, masculine styled wine; however, it lacks the sophistication and refinement of those of the northern Rhône. Judicious levels of acidity support a montage of exotic flavors. Look for blackberries, raspberries, cassis, plums, chocolate, leather, smoked meats, and spices (especially black pepper). Better vintages can age for 15-20 years. Quality can be high.

White Châteauneuf-du-Pape is made from a montage of southern Rhône grapes. It is a full-bodied wine loaded with fresh fruity flavors. The wine can be quite delicious; however, longevity is short.

Côtes du Rhône: The wine style is similar to Châteauneuf-du-Pap, but it is less concentrated and not as complex. However, some of the better wines can stand up to a good quality Châteauneuf-du-Pap.

Côtes du Rhône Villages: These wines are produced from a selected group of villages whose wines are of superior quality. They are richer, fuller, and have more concentrated and complex flavors than those labeled simply Côtes du Rhône. The village wines are worth a search as the price is not much different from the standard Côtes du Rhône bottling.

Beaumes de Venise: The little village of Beaumes de Venise produces red wines that are usually sold as a Côtes du Rhône. Its fame, however, comes from its dessert wine **Muscat de Beaumes de Venise**. These are very sweet fortified wines that have good acidity and lush, rich, concentrated and complex fruity flavors. Look for grapes, peaches, apples, apricots, pears, oranges, topical fruits, nuts, and honey. Drink these wines within their first 4-5 years.

Tavel: Only rosé wines are produced in this appellation. The wines are made from Grenache and a montage of other southern Rhône grapes. These dry, crisp, full-bodied wines have a beautiful ruby-orange color. Fresh, juicy, acidity bolsters loads of clean, fresh, fruity flavors. Drink Tavel young to enjoy its pristine freshness. Longevity is short but quality is high.

GERMANY

Ahh...Sehr gut!

Germany's noblest grape, the Riesling, is planted in only 20% of its vineyards. The most common varietal is the Müller-Thurgau, a high yielding grape of mediocre to good quality. The other common varietal, Sylvaner, usually produces flat, green flavored, prosy wines.

The punctilious precision of the German winemaker can be seen in the character of their wines. German wines are rigorously constructed over a framework of sweetness counterbalanced by crisp, clean acidity.

WINE CATEGORIES

There are two categories of quality German wines. Wines labeled **Qualitätswein (QbA)** are of lesser quality than those labeled **Qualitätswein mit Prädikat (QmP)**. QmP wines are further broken down into **Kabinett, Spätlese, Auslese, Beerenauslese (BA), and**

Trockenbeerenauslese (TBA). The chart below demonstrates the characteristics of each category. The wines become richer, sweeter and more flavorful as you progress from left to right.

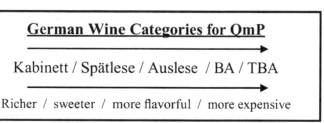

<u>**German Wine Categories for QmP**</u>

Kabinett / Spätlese / Auslese / BA / TBA

Richer / sweeter / more flavorful / more expensive

Figure 16 As you progress from left to right, the wines become richer, sweeter more flavorful and more expensive.

There is a fully dry styled German wine called **Trocken**, and a wine with just a token of sweetness called **Halbtrocken**. These are high acid wines, and because of their low level of alcohol and absence of sugar, Trocken wines are almost totally devoid of sweetness. This often causes a problem with balance, as the aggressiveness of acidity does not sufficiently counterbalance sweetness.

There are three styles of dessert wines made: **Beerenauslese, Trockenbeerenauslese (TBA), and Eiswein.** Beerenauslese and Trockenbeerenauslese are made from very ripe grapes, a high percentage of which are affected with a fungus called *Botrytis Cinerea.* The fungus attacks the grape skin and dehydrates the grape by making the skins permeable to water. Such grapes are said to have undergone "**noble rot**." This process concentrates the sugars, acids, alcohol, and flavorful extracts within the grape berry. In Germany the term for noble rot is called *edelfäule,* which is identical to the French term *pourriture noble.* Grapes affected with "noble rot" look terrible, but these affected grapes make outstanding dessert wines.

Beerenauslese wines are less rich and not quite as sweet as TBA's. They are made from selected grape berries, some of which may not be completely dehydrated. **Trockenbeerenauslese** wines are made from individually selected wizened grapes that have fully shriveled as a result of dehydration. These berries have high concentrations of sugars and extracts, and the resulting wines are very sweet. Both of these styles of wine have an exotic montage of rich, concentrated flavors. They are very expensive wines, but a little goes a long way.

Eiswein is one of the most unusual wines in the world. The secret in producing Eiswein is hang time on the vine. The berries are allowed to stay on the vine until frost. During that time they are subjected to predators, such as birds, and must be protected by nets or other devices. Eiswein is crisper and fresher and a little lighter and less sweet than either Beerenauslese or Trockenbeerenauslese.

There are eleven specified regions (called Anbaugebieten) whose wines are entitled to a Qualitätswein designation; however, we will consider only the six major growing areas. Each of these regions makes its own specific style of wine. Wine producing villages often have their village name incorporated into the name of their wines.

German wine labels can be very confusing and this is one of the chief obstacles in marketing their wine. The words are long and foreign, and the system is complicated. However, Germany is without question, the premier producer of this style of wine.

The highest quality wines are made from the Riesling grape. Such wines will invariably have the word "Riesling" printed somewhere on the label. If "Riesling" is not found on the label, there is a high probability that wine is made from Müller-Thurgau or Sylvaner grapes.

REGIONS

Classically, **Rhine wines are sold in brown, long-necked bottles and Mosel-Saar-Ruwer wines are packaged in long-necked green bottles.** However, there is a noticeable increase in the use of more eye-catching bottles that are used as a marketing ploy.

Mosel-Saar-Ruwer (M-S-R)

These are the lightest in both color and weight of all the German wines. They have a glimmering pale yellow color often with a hint of green. Clean, crisp, refreshing acidity bolsters a montage of delicate fruity flavors. Alcohol is in the range of 7-10%. Look for flavors of green apples, limes, lemons, peaches, grapes, minerals, honey and flowers. Some of the more famous wine producing villages are Piesporter, Wehlen, and Bernkastel. **Bernkastel Doktor** is the most famous wine from the region. Some of the wines will have a little **spritz** (slight carbonation), which adds to their charm.

Rhine Wines

Rheingau: These wines are richer, riper, and have a fuller body than the M-S-R wines. They have a shimmering golden color and a delicate perfumed nose. Alcohol is higher and the wines are not as tart as the M-S-R wines, but there is still plenty of mouthwatering acidity. Look for flavors of apples, peaches, grapes, oranges, lemons, limes, beeswax, minerals and honey. Some of the better vineyards include: **Schloss Vollrads, Schloss Johannisberg, Rauenthaler Baiken, Rüdesheimer Berg Schlossberg, Johannisberger Klaus,** and **Steinberg.**

Rheinhessen: Riesling is planted in only a small percentage of the vineyards from this region. Nevertheless, the wine is gifted with a soft delicate floral bouquet and rich, ripe, fruity flavors that are well focused and easy to perceive. Acidity is lower and the wines have less concentration than Rheingau wines. Look for flavors of flowers, honey, ripe apples, grapes, and minerals. The most famous village is Nierstein, whose name is attached to a great percentage of the wine produced. Some of the high quality estate-bottled wines include: **Oppenheimer Herrenberg, Mackenheimer Engelsberg, Binger Scharlachberg, Niersteiner Obel,** and **Niersteiner Hipping.** Most of the wine from this area is made from Müller-Thurgau and Sylvaner grapes and is marketed as **Liebfraumilch**. For the most part, these are inexpensive, prosy wines.

Nahe: These wines are styled similar to the M-S-R but are a little fuller bodied and a little less crisp. Look for flavors of apples, pears, peaches, grapes, flowers, honey, spices, and minerals. Notable villages include **Schlossböckelheim, Bad Kreuznach,** and **Niederhausen.**

Rheinpfalz: This region produces wines that have the deepest color and the fullest body of all the German wines. Acids are lower and alcohols are higher than in the other German regions. Look for flavors of apples, citrus, grapes, peaches, mangos, apricots, and honey. Many of the wines have a characteristic spicy earthy flavor. Two famous labels to look for are **Forster Jesuitengarten** and **Diedesheimer Hofstück.**

Franken: Wines from this region are made from the Sylvaner and Muller-Thurgau grapes. They are totally dry and have a characteristic earthy-vegetal taste. Other flavors include honey, citrus, apples, and minerals. The wines are sold in flattened flask shaped bottles called Bocksbeutels. The most famous wine is **Stein**.

ITALY

Chianti, mi amore?

In Italy there are so many different varietals and blends of wines under so many different names that it is impossible to cover the topic of Italian wines in anything short of a book. As you can imagine, the character and styles of the wine vary considerably, and there is not much of a bond that ties them together. The whites do have a few characteristics in common: most are light, tart, and have subdued flavors of almonds and citrus. The reds are generally tart and medium bodied. Other than these characteristics, there is great diversity in their make-up.

In the past, the Italian wine law placed its emphasis on quantity rather than quality. However, at the present time, this ideology is in a dynamic state of change, and the philosophy of wine makers is changing faster than the Italian wine law can cope.

Cabernet Sauvignon has taken a strong foothold, especially around Tuscany. Some of the Cabernet Sauvignon based wines are spectacular. Other Bordeaux blending grapes are also finding their way into Italian blends with very favorable results. As you might expect, the price of these wines is high—often too high.

Several notable grape varieties such as Chardonnay, Pinot Gris (called Pinot Grigio in Italy), Riesling, and Merlot are grown in many localities throughout the country. In general, these wines are tarter, lighter, and less concentrated than their California counterpart.

Many other famous wines have unusual names. Most are blends. In spite of their fanciful names (*Est! Est!! Est!!!, Lacryma Christi),* the majority is of average to poor quality. Nevertheless, quality in Italian wines is increasing, but so are the prices.

The Trebbiano grape is by far the most common white wine grape in Italy and a common ingredient in many of their blended wines. The grape is prolific and is found peppered throughout the countryside. This undistinguished grape produces a tart wine that is deficient in flavorful extracts and alcohol. To its credit, it does add tartness to the blend of an otherwise acid deficient wine, but at the same time, it dilutes the richness and flavors of the other varietals in the blend. Unfortunately, Trebbiano is even used as a blending agent in some red wines such as Chianti. The poor reputation of Italian white wines can be traced, at least in part to the inclusion of Trebbiano in the blend of their wines.

Veneto

Soave: This is a white wine made from the Garganega, Trebbiano, and recently Chardonnay grapes. The color is pale straw and the wine gives off little aroma. Acids are high, alcohol is low, and flavors are often fleeting: Look for almonds, apples, oranges, lemons, grapefruit, melon, pears, flowers, and herbs. Occasionally, good, sound, flavorful wines are produced. Drink young.

Bardolino: The color of this wine is just a shade deeper than rosé. The principal grape variety is the Corvina. The wine has high levels of refreshing acidity that support a good infusion of fruity extracts.

Look for scents and flavors of almonds, bitter lemon rind, strawberries, watermelon, cherries, berries, plums, apples, and oranges. This is an unsophisticated but refreshing wine. Drink young.

Valpolicella: This is nothing more than a richer and deeper colored Bardolino. Its moderately intense red color is accented with a slight orange cast. Flavors are similar to Bardolino but more concentrated. Look for almonds, raspberries, strawberries, cherries, plumbs, lemons, limes, spices, roses, anise, and tobacco. Drink young.

Amarone della Valpolicella: The principal grape variety is the Corvina. Ripe to overripe grapes are picked and hung to dry and shrivel. A large percentage of the grapes are affected with the fungus *Botrytis Cinerea*. These conditions concentrates the extracts in the grape.

The wine is garnet in color with noticeable brown tones at the edge. Alcohol and tannins are high, and there is a good complement of acidity that bolsters a variety of complex flavors. Look for dried fruits, plums, peaches, grapes, apples, almonds, flowers, smoke, coffee, and chocolate. Some of the wines can be quite impressive. The better wines can age for up to a decade or more. Poor wines are tannic and bitter.

Piedmont

Barolo: The Nebbiolo grape reaches its perfection in Barolo. The wine is inky dark with deep red-purple tones in the bowl and tawny highlights at the meniscus. In its youth, this is a hard, angular wine that should not be drunk for at least 10-12 years. Acids and tannins abound and alcohol is very high. At maturity the wine softens and develops a stunning montage of complex flavors and scents. Look for cassis, berries, cherries, smoke, tobacco, mushrooms, truffles, tar, saddle leather, violets, roses, pine, fennel, cedar, raisins, prunes, and exotic spices. The finish is a wonder—complex, concentrated, and phenomenally prolonged. Many connoisseurs consider this wine to be the most powerful of all dry table wines. High quality wines can last for decades.

Barbaresco: This wine is made from the same grape and in the same style as Barolo. However, it is usually a little lighter and less concentrated. In many years, you cannot tell the two apart.

Gattinara: This is a softer, lighter, and less sophisticated version of Barbaresco. It is made from the same grape (Nebbiolo) and has a similar flavor profile, but is less concentrated and complex.

Barbara: The name of the grape is the same as the wine; however, the wine always has a village name hyphenated to its name, such as Barbara d'Alba or Barbara d'Asti. It is a robust red wine, high in acidity (sometimes too high), but tannins are judiciously controlled. Flavors are characteristic for the varietal—cherries and dried fruits being particularly common. Most are of average quality.

Dolcetto: This is a ruby-purple colored wine made from the Dolcetto grape. Some refer to it as "Italy's Beaujolais' It has controlled acidity, but liberal amounts of soft tannins. Rich, ripe fruity flavors abound: look for almonds, strawberries, cherries, raspberries, blackberries, peaches, licorice, cinnamon, pepper, chocolate and minerals. Drink young.

Asti Spumante: This is a light, simply constructed sparkling wine that has a tendency to be cloyingly sweet. The mousse is unpolished, alcohol is low, and flavors are simple. Look for a grapy flavored wine seasoned with lemon and apple flavors. The wine is made from the Moscato di Canelli grape.

Cortese: Although relatively uncommon, Cortese is one of Italy's best wines. It is the name of the grape as well as the wine grape. Most are sold as Cortese del Piemonte, but wines of a little higher quality are labeled Cortese di Gavi or Cortese dell'Alto Monferrato. Flavors are delicate and acids are high. Look for apples, lemons, peaches, anise, and minerals. Drink young.

Tuscany

Chianti: This is a blended red wine that has considerable diversity of styles and quality. Sangiovese is the predominant varietal in the blend, and its character dominates the wine. Look for a medium weight wine of somewhat limited concentration with a good core of acidity and moderate amounts of alcohol.

Most of the wines are no better than average. Nonetheless, some wines are superb: rich, sophisticated, elegant, and gifted with an array of complex Sangiovese varietal flavors. Look for raspberries, blackberries, strawberries, cassis, cherries, plums, spice, smoke, chocolate, leather, and tar. The average Chianti should be consumed in 3-4 years. Reserve wines are generally of higher quality, the better of which can last for a dozen years or more.

Brunello di Montalcino: This wine is made from a superior clone of Sangiovese called the Sangiovese Grosso. These are big, rich, and powerful red wines that are full-bodied, tannic, and tart. It takes several years for them to soften sufficiently enough to expose their parade of concentrated and complex scents and flavors. If balanced, these can be outstanding wines—one of Italy's best; however, many have a problem with balance being too tart or too tannic. Look for scents and flavors of cherries, raspberries, plums, anise, spice, prunes, coffee, tar, truffles, licorice, and chocolate.

Super Tuscans: These are the new super stars in the Italian wine industry. Super Tuscans are typically made of a blend composed of some combination of the classic Bordeaux grape varieties and Sangiovese. However, some are single varietals such as pure Cabernet Sauvignon. The characteristics of the wine parallel the varietal character of the grapes in the blend. Super Tuscans are now receiving their own appellation.

Vernaccia di San Gimignano: This is a pale, dry white wine made from the Vernaccia grape. It can be made full-bodied or in a lighter style. Typically the wine is dry, crisp, fresh, and fruity. Flavors include almonds, pears, lemons, apples, honey, and a hint of varnish, which in no way detracts from the character of the wine. Drink this wine young.

Carmignano: Similar to Chianti but blended with up to 10% Cabernet Sauvignon, this wine has a little more depth and sophistication than a typical Chianti.

Abruzzi

Montepulciano d'Abruzzo: This is a simple everyday red wine that lacks refinement, sophistication, and complexity, yet it has a good dose of fruity flavors supported by solid acidity. Look for flavors of plums, berries, cedar, coffee, pepper, leather, tobacco, and earth. Occasionally the grape can be coached in producing surprisingly good wines.

Latium

Frascati: These are average quality white wines that have good crisp acidity, light body, and delicate fruity flavors. The wines are a blend of Malvasia and Trebbiano. Look for lemon, pear, melon, peaches, tangerines, spices, herbs, nuts, and flowers.

Est! Est!! Est!!! – The name is more colorful than the wine. This white wine is made from the same grapes as Frascati. Quality, structure, and flavors are also similar.

Marches

Verdicchio: This white wine is produced principally from the Verdicchio grape blended with smaller amounts of Malvasia and Trebbiano. Look for a light-bodied, high acid wine with delicate scents and flavors: apples, lemons, nuts, and smoke.

Umbria

Orvieto: Grechetto, Trebbiano, and Verdello grapes make up the blend of this white wine. It is usually dry, but can be sweet. Typically, this is a somewhat drab, light-bodied wine of medium acidity that has poorly concentrated flavorful extracts: nuts, apples, flowers, and smoke. Many of the wines are oxidized by the time they are purchased. Occasionally, surprisingly good quality wines are produced.

Campania

Lacryma Christi: The name means "tears of Christ." This white wine, made from the Greco della Torre grape, is smooth, dry, and of ordinary quality. Look for delicate flavors of almonds, apples and flowers. Drink on release.

Greco di Tufo: This is a ripe, round, full-bodied white wine with medium acidity made from Greco grapes that are grown around the village of Tufo. Look for flavors of apples, peaches, pears, oranges, anise, minerals, herbs, flowers, and nuts. Quality is average to good.

NEW ZEALAND

With the production of its uniquely styled Sauvignon Blanc, New Zealand suddenly attained a solid foothold onto the world wine stage. The cool maritime climate and favorable soil conditions are ideal for the production of Chardonnay and Sauvignon Blanc. Fairly good Rieslings are also produced. The weather and soil seem to be perfect for Pinot Noir; however, in spite of a few exemplary wines with good Burgundian traits, the region is struggling with this varietal. The industry is also starting to produce surprisingly good Cabernet Sauvignon and Merlot. Nevertheless, it is the white wines that New Zealand is famous for, and there is no doubt that the superstar of the industry is Sauvignon Blanc.

Sauvignon Blanc: This unoaked and unblended wine is the quintessence of white wines from the region. It is light-moderate weight and is gifted with an array of fruity-green flavors. Look for gooseberry, blackcurrants, citrus, grass, green vegetables, and a dash of herbs. New Zealand Sauvignon Blanc is a great food wine and will pair with an array of vegetables such as asparagus, fennel, parsnips, and green beans.

***Chardonnay*:** These are streamlined, Burgundian styled wines with good crisp acidity and clean, vibrant, fresh fruity flavors. There is less weight and less tropical fruit flavors than those produced in Australian and California. Look for flavors of nuts, grapefruit, lemon, melon, and spices. Their lighter weight and good crisp acidity makes them easy to match to a wide variety of foods.

PORTUGAL

Portugal's dry red table wine industry has blossomed over the past few years. Unlike most other countries that rely on familiar varietals like Cabernet Sauvignon, Syrah and Merlot, Portugal's dry reds are made from little known native grape varietals such as Touriga Nacional, Tinta Roriz (Tempranillo), Touriga Franca, and Tinta Amarela. The best wines are rich and full-bodied. Because of the diversity of grape varieties, it is difficult to profile these wines. Common flavors include cherries, plums, blackberries and raspberries, smoke, spice, grilled meats and tar.

Although Portugal is more famous for its reds, there is one noteworthy white wine, Vinho Verde, which you can occasionally find outside of Portugal. This is a light-bodied wine with clean, crisp acidity that supports delicate, spicy-fruity flavors. The interesting aspect of the wine is that it has just a hint of sparkle (spritz) due to a small residual of carbon dioxide gas remaining in bottle after malolactic fermentation.

Port

Port is a sweet, fortified dessert wine. **Fortified** wines have their alcohol content increased by the addition of alcohol, usually in the form of brandy. There are four main divisions of Port: White Port, Ruby Port, Vintage Port, and Tawny Port. Except for white Port, they are all made from the same montage of grapes, but are vinified by radically different methods

- ***White Port***: This golden colored wine is made from a blend of unfamiliar white grapes. It can be dry or sweet. Most are of average quality.

- ***Vintage Port***: This wine represents the crescendo of Port styles. Dozens of grape varietals go into the production of Port. When a particular vintage has outstanding qualities, a vintage year is declared. This occurs about every three years. Vintage Ports are aged in wood for two years, but then must be aged in bottle for a decade or more before they are ready for consumption. Vintage Ports are very full-bodied fortified wines with rich, sweet, and powerful flavors. Although they are sweet, they are rarely cloying. The wine gets smoother and more polished the longer it ages in bottle. Flavors are intense. It is a wonder that so much fruit remains after a 20 or 30-year repose in bottle. Alcohol levels are around 20%.

Look for flavors of blackberries, raspberries, blackcurrants, cherries, grapes, plums, flowers, figs, dried fruits, raisins, licorice, tar, tobacco, truffles, herbs, spices, chocolate, and nuts.

Vintage Port develops dense sediment that requires decanting. Once opened, these wines must be consumed. Because of these qualities, they are poor wines to be sold by the glass in restaurants. Beware of restaurants that serve Vintage Port by the glass.

An alternative is the modern version of **Late Bottled Vintage Port**. While not a true Vintage Port, they are good sound wines that have a structure similar to Vintage Port but are less refined and sophisticated. They do not throw sediment, and can last for several weeks after opening. ***Vintage Character Port*** is nothing more than a high quality Ruby Port that attempts to resemble Vintage Port. It is yet another name often confused with Vintage Port. **Single Quinta Vintage Ports** are wines from a single estate whose grapes come from selected high quality properties in non-vintage years. They are structured similar to Vintage Port, but are of less quality.

• ***Tawny Port***: This wine develops its tawny color by being aged in wood for 10-20 years or more. They are lighter and more delicate than Vintage Port. Look for flavors of cherries, nuts, raisins, caramel, and leather.

• ***Colheita Port***: Similar to Tawny Port, but made from a single vintage. The vintage year is printed on the label, which makes for some confusion with Vintage Port.

• ***Ruby Port***: In average years, much of the vintage goes into the production of Ruby Port. The wine is matured in wood for three years and then bottled. It is a somewhat rough wine that lacks polish and sophistication. Ruby Port does not improve in bottle, but will keep for several months after opening.

Madeira

Madeira: This is a unique wine made in the Portuguese island of Madeira. The vinification process is extremely unusual. The must is baked in glass-lined vats for three to four months and then aged in a Solera (see Sherry), so there are no vintage dates. Most are named after the grapes that create the diversity of its styles. The majority is made from white grapes.

Sercial is pale golden, light, fresh, tangy, and dry. These are great apéritif wines.

Verdelho is amber-brown in color, medium-dry, and softer than Sercial.

Rainwater is similar to Verdelho, but very light in color.

Bual is medium-sweet and dark amber in colored. It is richer, and more concentrated than Verdelho.

Malmsey is made from the Malvasia grape. It is dark brown, very rich and sweet, and very concentrated. This wine makes a great finish to an evening meal.

Terrantez is now difficult to find. It is medium sweet, tart, and very fragrant.

Bastardo is another disappearing variety that is made from a red grape. They are dark brown in color, rich, and full-bodied.

There are several other types made from a variety of grapes, but these are the ones that you are likely to run into.

Although these wines are made from different grape varietals, a unique tangy, volcanic, scorched sugar and caramel flavor tie them together. Other flavors include peaches, cognac, violets, toffee, vanilla, coffee, nuts and chocolate. With age, quality wines develop a distinctive green cast at the rim of the glass.

SOUTH AFRICA

There is considerable wine making potential in this country that has not been tapped. South Africa has only recently begun to develop its table wine industry, but several outstanding wines are being produced. With the exception of costal and mountainous regions, the climate is warm and dry. The following is a description of the popular varietals:

- **Chenin Blanc**: This grape, which in South Africa is called *Steen*, is the dominant varietal in this country accounting for about 1/3 of the total plantings. It is primarily used to make medium-dry to semi-sweet wines. Some good sparkling wines and late harvest wines are also produced.

- **Cinsaut** is the same grape as Cinsault from the Rhone Valley and is the leading red varietal. In South Africa it is called **Hermitage**. The grape produces a spectrum of wine from rosés to full, rich, fruity red wines. An unusual scent of raw meat is a characteristic marker for the wine.

- **Pinotage**: This grape, a hybrid cross between Pinot Noir and Cinsault, is unique to South Africa. It is an easy drinking, inexpensive wine that has a cherry-earthy flavor. Some can be quite delicious.

- **Cabernet Sauvignon, Pinot Noir, and Shiraz** are up-and-coming red wines. Cabernet Sauvignon is particularly successful.

- **Sauvignon Blanc and Chardonnay** are becoming increasingly important among the white varietals. Sauvignon Blanc, made in an unusually assertive style, is particularly successful.

SPAIN

Spain is best known for Sherry; however, many table wines of outstanding quality are produced throughout the region. The introduction of Cabernet Sauvignon and Chardonnay grapes into the viniculture of Spain gives the region great promise. These grapes interact favorably with the soil and climate of Spain, and are being planted in increasing numbers throughout the country.

Although the country is beginning to produce good quality white wines, most are of average quality. Spain has a wide spectrum of good quality native white grapes, such as Albarino and Verdejo, but the introduction of Chardonnay and Sauvignon Blanc will undoubtedly encourage the upward trend in white wine quality. Spain does, however, produce some outstanding red wines; some of these reds are classics.

You might find the names of Spanish wines very confusing, because they come from little known areas and are made of grapes with foreign names. It is not within the scope of this book to delve into the intricacies of these wines, but the following paragraphs will give you a general outline of the more important areas.

Table Wines

Rioja: This is the most famous table wines district in Spain. It is divided into three parts. **Rioja Alta** is planted mostly with Tempranillo and produces the best wines or the region . **Rioja Alavesa** wines are similar to Rioja Alta, but less sophisticated. **Rioja Baja** are made almost entirely from Garnacha (Grenache) and are the heaviest and least refined of the threesome.

Although most of the wines are a blend of Tempranillo and Garnacha, plantings of Cabernet Sauvignon are on the upswing. The better wines are medium to full-bodied with moderate alcohol levels and soft well-behaved tannins. Rioja wines are gentle, velvety, and rich. Acidity is tempered, but sufficient to shores up a bevy of concentrated flavors. Look for scents and savors of cherries, boysenberries, plums, prunes, smoke, tobacco, chocolate, coffee, licorice, leather, and spice. Some of the better producers include:

La Rioja Alta, CVNE, Muga, Remelluri, and **Bilbainas.** The average wine should be drunk within 5-6 years. Great wines can last for a decade or two. This area is presently in a state of flux. New winemaking techniques are being introduced and more traditional grape varieties are being planted.

Penedès: There is an assortment of grapes that go into the blend of the wines from this region, which makes description of their character somewhat difficult. In general they are solid, hefty wines with deeply concentrated flavors and soft tannins. The most famous wines from the region are **Torres, Gran Coronas Black Label** made from Cabernet Sauvignon, and **Torres Gran Coronas Reserva,** a blend of Cabernet Sauvignon and Merlot. The area is also famous for an inexpensive wine with a flashy name called **Sangre de Toro,** or "Bull's Blood." Most of Spain's sparkling wines are also produced in this region

Ribera del Duero: The Tempranillo grapes in this area have mutated and are known as Tinto Fino. These grapes produce fuller-bodied and more intense wines than what would be expected from the Tempranillo found in Rioja. These are powerful, complex, and deeply concentrated wines. The two most famous wines are **Pesquera**, made from Tinto Fino, and **Vega Sicilia Uneco**, a legendary wine made from Cabernet Sauvignon, Merlot, Malbec and an undisclosed amount of Tinto Fino. Although the wine is outstanding, it is prohibitively expensive. More affordable wines from **Vega Sicilia** are **Tinto Valbuena** and **Valbuena.**

Toro: Most of the wines are blends of Tempranillo (known locally as Tinta de Toro) and Grenache. They are powerful, hearty, full-bodied wines that are high in alcohol. Judicious levels of acidity sustain an assortment of concentrated and complex flavors. The wines have a rustic character and lack somewhat in sophistication and finesse; nonetheless, they are quality wines that represent good values.

Rueda: **Verdejo**, one of Spain's best white wines is produced in this region. It is a streamlined, fruity wine with a good complement of fruit supporting acidity.

Navarra: This area has improved its viniculture quite dramatically over the past several years. The wines are made from a mixture of old traditional Spanish varietals (predominantly Garnacha and Tempranillo) blended with more traditional varietals: Cabernet Sauvignon, Syrah, Merlot, and Chardonnay.

Somontano: This is another area in Spain that has significantly improved its winemaking ability. Formerly an area of mediocrity, it is now producing many high quality wines that are sold at bargain prices. These are deep colored, full-bodied red wines made from an assortment of Bordeaux varietals often blended with Tempranillo and Granacha. Some very good Chardonnays are also produced.

Priorato: This region is making some of the most exciting and expensive wines in Spain. The wines are hefty, full-bodied, high in alcohol, and deep in color. These age-worthy wines have an aggressive peppery flavor and in many ways are similar to the red Rhônes. Garnacha is the principle grape that is usually blended with Cabernet Sauvignon, Syrah and Merlot.

Galicia: The fame of this area is due to the production of **Albarino**, a white wine with very high acidity and a delicate fruity, floral flavor. It is one of Spain's best wines made from native grapes. Bodegas Morgadia is the best producer of this wine.

Sherry

Sherry is the great fortified wine of Spain. There are two main divisions of Sherry: **Fino** and **Oloroso**. Sherry wines have no vintage dates because quality is maintained year after year by a unique process called the **solera system**. In this system, wines are stacked in barrels one on top of the other. The youngest wines are placed in the top barrels and as you go down the sequence to the bottom barrels the wines get progressively older. Wines for bottling are drawn from the bottom barrel, and no more than one-third of the volume is removed. The volume is replaced by slightly younger wine from the next barrel up. This process continues up the chain of barrels to the top barrel. The top barrel's volume is replaced by an intermediate solera that has undergone a similar evolutionary process.

These are the main styles

- *Fino* is pale yellow in color and has a fine bouquet. On the palate, the wine is very dry, crisp, and appears lighter than you might expect from a wine with an alcohol level of around 16-17%. A great part of the flavor is derived from the yeast (flor) that forms on the surface of open vats of the wine. Its unique flavor is impossible to describe and must be experienced. Additional savors include yeast, nuts, sweet hay, and spices. The sole grape in its production is the Palomino. The wine should be drunk young and lasts only a day or two after opening.

- *Manzanillas* are Finos from the fishing port of Sanlúcar de Barrameda. They have the flavors of Fino with a sharp, tangy salty note.

- *Amontillado* is a Fino aged in wood that has lost its flor. It is darker in color and richer in body than classical Fino. Acidity is less than the other categories of Fino and the flavors are more concentrated.

The distinguishing feature of this wine is its rich nutty flavor. Most Amontillados are sweetened with **Pedro Ximénez**, a cloyingly sweet wine mainly used as a blending wine to add sweetness.

- *Oloroso* is aged in wood and not exposed to air as in the production of Fino. It has a golden brown color, a fragrant nose, and is heavier, richer, and softer than Fino. Alcohol levels of 18-19%, gives these wines a rich, full-body and a gentle, warm mouth feel. Look for flavors of nuts, raisins, dried fruits, toffee, brown sugar, butterscotch, caramel, and molasses. The dry wine is made exclusively from the Palomino grape; however, many wines are sweetened with Pedro Ximénez.

- *Palo Cortado* is an uncommon Sherry that is structured like Oloroso but has the aroma of Amontillado.

- *Cream Sherry* is a generic name for a smooth sweet Sherry that contains about 19% alcohol and about 13 % sugar. Cream Sherry is an Oloroso sweetened with large amounts of Pedro Ximénez, which often makes it cloyingly sweet.

- *Pedro Ximénez (PX)*: This is the name of the grape as well as the wine. It is a very sweet and full-bodied wine that has a flavor of dried fruit—especially raisins. It is one of the richest and sweetest of the dessert wines. The sweet richness of the wine together with the lack of counterbalancing acidity tends to make the wine cloying. PX is primarily used as a blending wine used to sweeten Sherry.

- *Malaga*: Pedro Ximénez and Moscatel grape make the golden brown, rich, and very sweet wines around the city of Malaga.

Quiz

Tip: Don't let the fancy wine names trip you up. Rather, use your knowledge of the grape varieties that make up these wines. Don't be discouraged if you miss a few; quizzes are learning experiences.

Multiple Choice

1. Which wine has the greater acidity? (a) Pinot Gris, (b) Gewurztraminer, (c) Viognier, (d) Trebbiano

2. Which wine has the fuller body? (a) Soave, (b) Australian Chardonnay, (c) California Sauvignon Blanc, (d) white Bordeaux

3. Which wine does not contain Cabernet Sauvignon? (a) red Bordeaux, (b) Chinon, (c) Torres, Grand Coronas Black Label, (d) Château Latour

4. Which wine typically has more tannin? (a) Barbaresco, (b) Gattinara, (c) Valpolicella, (d) Oregon Pinot Noir.

5. Which wine will have more tannin? (a) 1955 Château Mouton Rothschild, (b) 1955 Château Haut Brion, (c) 2001 Ravenswood Rancho Salina, Cabernet Sauvignon, (d) 1999 Ponzi Pinot Noir

6. Which wine will be dominated by fresh, ripe, fruity flavors? (a) 2001 Fritz Haag, Brauneberger Juffer Sonnenuhr Spätlese, (b) 1980 Sancerre, (c) 1970 Château Cheval Blanc, (d) Lustau, Fino Sherry

7. This tart and tannic wine has flavors of black currant, cedar, and spices. It is most likely (a) 1998 Gevrey-Chambertin, (b) 2000 Villa Mt. Eden Chardonnay, (c) 1997 Kendall Jackson Cabernet Sauvignon, (d) 1999 Rex Hill Pinot Noir

8. This sweet fortified wine has flavors of berries, cherries, plums, figs, licorice, tobacco, spices and nuts. It is most likely (a) Churchill's Agua Alta Vintage Port 1990. (b) Alvear Fino

Sherry, (c)Henriques & Henriques Sercial Madiera, 10 year, (d) Milz, Trittenheimer Apotheke Eiswein.

9. Which of the following wines will have the darkest color? (a) 2001 Corton Charlemagne, (b) 1990 Mommessin, Clos de Tart red Burgundy, (c) 1999 Château Latour, (d) George Duboeuf, Fleurie 2000.

10. This thick and oily feeling wine has low acidity and a rich full body. Flavors are pronounced and distinct: lichee nuts, rose petals, and grapefruit. The most likely choice is: (a) Alfred Merkelbach, Kinheimer Rosenberg Kabinett, M-S-R 2000, (b) Guigal Condrieu Luminescence 2000, (c) Zind-Humbrecht Goldert V.T. Gewurztraminer 1999, (d) Weinbach Cuvee Theo 1999 Riesling.

11. This is a soft, supple, and rich wine that has flavors of beetroot, cherries, smoky meats, and spices. Both acids and tannins are restrained. The best choice would be (a) 2000 Lindemans Australian Chardonnay. (b) 2000 Domaine du Vissoux Moulin a Vent (Beaujolais), (c) 1999 Nicolas Potel Clos Vougeot, (d) 2002 Antinori Castello di Brolio Chianti Classico.

12. Sauvignon Blanc's varietal character is best expressed by (a) white Bordeaux, (b) California Sauvignon Blanc, (c) Pouilly-Fumé, (d) Pouilly-Fuissé

Answers

1. (d) Trebbiano

2. **(b) Australian Chardonnay:** This wine is noted for its rich full-body

3. **(b) Chinon**

4. **(a) Barbaresco**

5. **(c) 2001 Ravenswood Rancho Salina, Cabernet Sauvignon**: Both 1955 wines will be low in tannins because tannins decrease as a wine ages. Pinot Noir has less tannin than Cabernet Sauvignon.

6. **(a) 1999 Fritz Haag, Brauneberger Juffer Sonnenuhr Spätlese**: The 1980 Sancerre will be oxidized and devoid of fruit because it is too old. The 1970 Cheval Blanc will have lost most of its aroma; instead, it will have the non-fruity scents of bouquet. Fino Sherry has limited fruit in its flavor profile, whereas the Spätlese abounds with fresh fruity flavors.

7. **(c) 1997 Kendall Jackson Cabernet Sauvignon**: This is the perfect description of a typical Cabernet Sauvignon.

8. **(a) Churchill's Agua Alta Vintage Port 1990**: Fino Sherry and Sercial Madeira are dry wines. Eiswein is not fortified.

9. **(c) 1995 Château Latour**: Corton Charlemagne is a white Burgundy. Red Burgundy (Pinot Noir) and Fleurie (Beaujolais) have only moderate color intensity. Château Latour, a Cabernet Sauvignon based wine is noted for its broodingly deep color.

10. **(c) Zind-Humbrecht Goldert V.T. 1999 Gewürztraminer**: Condrieu is made from Viognier. The flavors of Viognier and Gewürztraminer are similar and both are full-bodied; however, Viognier is very delicate and introspective. Gewürztraminer is an extrovert with big, bold flavors. The M-S-R and the Alsatian Riesling are both high acid wines.

11. **(c) 1995 Nicolas Potel Clos Vougeot**: This is a typical description for red Burgundy (Pinot Noir).

12. **(c) Pouilly-Fumé**: Pouilly-Fuissé is made from Chardonnay grapes. White Bordeaux and California Sauvignon Blanc are wines that are oaked and blended with Semillon and these ministrations will alter the structure and flavor profile of Sauvignon Blanc. Pouilly-Fumé is made from pure unadulterated Sauvignon Blanc.

Part 2

Matching Wine with Food

MATCHING WINE WITH FOOD

"Lester, why did you wear that awful checkered jacket? ...And that calico shirt, it doesn't match at all!"

Matching wine with food will be simple now that you have an understanding of wine. This part of the book will give you a logical method for matching a wine with food. You will not see long lists of wine-food parings, which are the core of many books relating to this topic. Such lists are not only incomplete, but they are often devoid of logic. The wine-food selections of one author will invariably differ from that of another. They may both have made sound selections, but the disparity in wine selection generates confusion.

This book deals with concepts, rather than lists of wine food pairings. The principles are logical and simple to understand. Once you have mastered the concepts, matching a wine with food will be easy.

Many of the concepts that relate to wine-food pairings you have already met when you learned about wine in the first part of this book. There are many parallelisms in wine that relate to food:

- Acidity supports and perks up flavors in wine; acidity also perks up the flavors in food. A crisp tart wine will perk-up the flavors in the majority of foods.

- Acidity lightens the weight and richness in wines; acidity does the same for food. An acid wine served with a rich food will lighten the weight of the food and decrease its richness. Acidifying food products, such as pickling, also lighten their weight. Acidic wines are great foils for ponderously heavy foods.

- The tannins in wine cover over many of its delicate flavors; tannins will also obscure delicate flavors in food. If you serve a tannic wine with a delicately flavored food, you will obscure many of its subtle flavors.

- Tannin's astringency is due to its ability to coagulate the slippery mucoproteins of the mouth; tannin similarly react with proteins in food, lightening them and making food more digestible. Big heavy, rich foods will be lightened if you pair them with a tannic wine.

- A dominant powerful flavor in a wine, such as oak, can snuff out a wines more subtle and delicate flavors; the same principle holds true for food. Wines with big, robust flavors will snuff out the flavors in delicately flavored foods.

- Sweetness subdues and counterbalances the aggressive elements in wine; in like fashion, sweetness will subdue the aggressive elements in food. Tart foods and hot spicy foods are assuaged by serving them with a sweet wine.

General Concept

Once you understand wine, matching wine with food is easy. The problem with most wine-food books is that they try to explain the general concepts of wine-food paring without providing a firm foundation in regard to the structure of wine. You cannot logically match wine to food unless you first understand wine. We all understand food; we've been eating since the day that we were born. Understanding wine is a newer discipline and a little more difficult to grasp.

If the fingers of your right hand represent the characteristics of wine, and the fingers of your left hand represent the characteristics of food, the idea in wine food pairing is to bring your fingers together in such fashion that they mirror each other. Sweet in wine matches to sweet in food, tart to tart, weight to weight, flavor to flavor, ethnicity to ethnicity, texture to texture, etc. This portion of the book goes into the nitty-gritty of how we accomplishing these pairings.

CHAPTER 8
Acidity

High Acid Wines

If you serve an acid wine with food, you will be well on your way to making a correct wine-food match for most dishes. Acids support flavor. Supplying acidity to a food has the same effect as salting your foods—it brings out flavor. Think of all the foods that are improved with a little splash of vinegar or a squeeze of lemon. Many of the condiments and sauces that are used to heighten the flavors in food are high in acids: catsup, salad dressings, vinegar, steak sauces, barbecue sauce, red pasta sauce, and pickle relish are common examples.

I have devised a test, which I call the **squeeze of lemon test** that will help determine which foods will benefit from an acid wine. It requires a little mental gymnastics, but if positive, will determine that the food in question will pair successfully with an acid wine.

The test is simple. If in your mind's eye, a few drops of freshly squeezed lemon juice will benefit the food in question, the dish will pair successfully to an acid wine. Will sautéed flounder benefit from a few drops of lemon juice? You bet it would. How about oysters on the half shell? A wedge of lemon is the perfect accompaniment. Unfortunately, some foods will have a negative test, and will still benefit from an acid wine. The test is only useful if it is positive.

Another trick is to look at classical preparations of specific food items that have tartness as part of their preparation such as lemon chicken, spaghetti and red sauce, sauerbraten (pickled pot roast), German potato salad (seasoned with vinegar and bacon), hot dogs and pickle relish, turkey and cranberry sauce, sweet and sour pork, shrimp and cocktail sauce, lemon buttered sole, and the list goes on. All of these foods are successfully paired to acidic elements. What this tells us is that red meats, white meats, starchy foods, shellfish, and fish all go well in an acid medium, and in the majority of instances will be benefited by the tartness in a crisp acidic wine. You can see that the classic food combinations, which have evolved down through the centuries, can give us great insight to what kind of wine will work with specific dishes.

However, sauces or other interactive ingredients can change the nature of the basic food product so that they may not work as well with an acid wine. Creamy or buttery foods that have a sense of lightness will frequently call for wine with round, soft features such as Chardonnay or Viognier. However, you will see as we go on in future chapters that rich, heavy, creamy foods will often need acidity or tannins to counter their richness, as the wine-food combination may become to cloyingly heavy.

When in doubt as to what kind of wine will go with a particular dish, you are always better off choosing an acid wine. The majority of food preparations will be improved by the acidity of a sound, tart wine.

The charts below outline the relative tartness of some of the commoner wines. Keep in mind that **young wines have more acidity than older wines**.

High Acid Wines	
White	*Red*
Champagne	Cabernet Sauvignon
Riesling	Syrah
Sauvignon Blanc	Sangiovese
Chablis	Barbara
Trebbiano	Gamay
Most Italian Whites	Nebbiolo
	Bordeaux
	Most Italian Reds
	Beaujolais

Low Acid Wines	
White	*Red*
Gewurztraminer	Merlot
Pinot Gris	Pinot Noir
California and Australian Chardonnay	Tempranillo
Viognier	Zinfandel
	Burgundy

Quiz

Will an acidic wine benefit the following dishes?

1. Grilled swordfish steak and herb buttered rice
2. Roast chicken and baked potato
3. Lobster and melted butter
4. Corn on the cob served with melted butter
5. Baked macaroni
6. Oysters on the half-shell
7. Cream based oyster stew
8. Frog legs and potato cakes
9. Hamburger and French fries
10. Crown roast of pork with boiled potatoes and gravy
11. Pizza
12. Chicken Pot Pie
13. Grilled Porterhouse steak
14. Spareribs
15. Shrimp with red cocktail sauce

Answers

1. **Grilled swordfish steak and herb buttered rice:** Yes. This dish has a positive squeeze of lemon test.

2. **Roast chicken and baked potato**: Yes. Classical food combinations tell us that poultry has an affinity for acidity: lemon chicken, turkey with cranberry sauce, etc.

3. **Lobster and melted butter**: Yes. This dish has a positive squeeze of lemon test.

4. **Corn on the cob served with melted butter**: No. Corn on the cob with butter has a negative squeeze of lemon test. This is a dish with a round, buttery mouth feel. This dish would not be enhanced by the tartness of lemon juice. Can you think of anything tart that you could combine with this dish to enhance it? Rather the dish is looking for a wine with a round, soft, mouth feel. A buttery Chardonnay would make a perfect match.

5. **Baked macaroni**: Yes. At first you might think that dishes such as baked macaroni might not benefit from an acid wine. You certainly don't squeeze lemon juice on top of macaroni. However, macaroni is pasta, and pasta certainly goes with tomato sauce—a tart red sauce. In fact, cooks will frequently put tomatoes in their baked macaroni. The rich cheesy sauce combined with the thick feel of pasta is heavy indeed. A big, heavy dish matched to a full-bodied, low-acid wine, would likely make the combination cloyingly heavy. You would need the relief of acids or tannins to lighten such a combination. It therefore follows that baked macaroni will be benefited by acidity, and a tart wine would be a very good accompaniment.

6. **Oysters on the half-shell**: Yes: This dish has a positive squeeze of lemon test.

7. **Cream based oyster stew**: You will need a creamy and tart wine! Oyster stew has a negative squeeze of lemon test. Have you ever seen a wedge of lemon served with oyster stew?

However, oysters themselves are benefited by a squeeze of lemon—tartness, while the creaminess of the stew is looking for round and creamy—not tart, sharp, and aggressive. Give the dish what it is looking for. A good quality Champagne would make an excellent match. Champagne is creamy and tart. The rich creamy bubbles in Champagne supply the round creaminess and the still wine provides plenty of tartness. The creaminess ties into the creamy base of the stew, while the tartness perks up the flavor of the oysters

8. **Frog legs and potato cakes**: Yes, Frog legs are similar to chicken, and chicken pairs well with tart wines.

9. **Hamburger and French fries**: Yes. You don't squeeze lemon on top of hamburger, but you put catsup and pickle relish on top of hamburgers; both of these are tart condiments. A good tart wine, perhaps Beaujolais, would make a great match.

10. **Crown roast of pork with boiled potatoes and gravy**: Yes. Acidity enlivens the flavor of pork; think of dishes such as sweet and sour pork and pork served with a tart applesauce.

11. **Pizza**: Yes. The tomato sauce on the pizza perks up its flavor, so will a tart wine. If you have tartness in a dish, you should have equal or greater tartness in the accompanying wine.

12. **Chicken Pot Pie**: Yes, same reason as question #2.

13. **Grilled Porterhouse steak**: Yes. A tart steak sauce enhances the flavor of steak. Therefore, a tart wine will likewise intensify the flavor in steak.

14. **Spareribs**: Yes. Spareribs are enhanced with tart barbecue sauce. Their flavor will likewise be enlivened with the acidity of a tart wine. Moreover, the tartness in the wine will cut the heavy, greasy character of the food.

15. **Shrimp with red cocktail sauce:** Yes. The dish has a positive squeeze of lemon test.

High Acid Foods

The only caveat when it comes to pairing a wine to a tart food is to make sure that the acidity of the wine is always equal to or greater than the acidity of the accompanying food. The mind subconsciously sets up a comparison between the tartness of the wine and that of the food. If the food is more acidic than the wine, it will make the wine appear flat and out of balance. The food will corrupt the wine! **Always keep the tartness in the wine greater than or equal to the tartness of the food.**

When you have an acid wine paired to an acid food, the degree of tartness appreciated is related to the difference between the tartness of the food and the tartness of the wine. A tart wine married to a tart food will appear to have less apparent tartness than the same tart wine married to a less tart food. The tartness in the wine and food do not add up as you might expect; it is the difference between the acidity of the wine to that of the food that stands out as you sip the wine.

Quiz

Which of the following wine-food pairings would you consider successful?

---

1. Chablis with Oysters
2. Viognier with sweet and sour pork
3. Alsatian Gewürztraminer with sauerbraten (German pickled pot roast)
4. Mature Merlot with roast pork topped with a tart cranberry flavored barbecue sauce
5. Barbara with spaghetti and meatballs

6. Sauvignon Blanc with grilled flounder topped with lemon dill sauce

7. Beaujolais with Polish sausage and sauerkraut

8. Cortese de Gavi (tart Italian wine) with shrimp scampi (shrimp with a garlic flavored sauce)

9. Riesling Kabinett served with grilled chicken topped with a sweet and tart pineapple-lemon relish

10. Pinot Grigio (Italian white) served with grilled chicken topped with tart apple-lemon relish

Answers

1. **Chablis with Oysters**: This is a wonderful match. The dish has a positive squeeze of lemon test, and Chablis is a tart white wine.

2. **Viognier with sweet and sour pork**: What a disaster. Viognier is a wine that lacks acidity. The wine will taste flat and out of balance when paired to the tartness in sweet and sour pork.

3. **Alsatian Gewürztraminer with sauerbraten (German pickled pot roast)**: Same situation as #2. Gewürztraminer lacks acidity. The tartness of sauerbraten will make the wine taste flat.

4. **Mature Merlot with roast pork topped with a tart cranberry barbecue sauce**: Poor choice. Same reasons as #2 and #3. Merlot is naturally low in acidity; at maturity it will be even lower. The cranberry barbecue sauce is tart and will make the wine appear out of balance. However, some youthful Merlot wines may have enough acidity to stand up to the dish, but they would not be first choice.

5. **Barbara with spaghetti and meatballs**: Barbara is a rustic, tart wine that will not be intimidated by the tartness of the tomato based spaghetti sauce. This is a very good match.

6. **Sauvignon Blanc with grilled flounder topped with lemon dill sauce**: This is a good match; the acidity of the wine is

greater than or equal to that of the dish. In addition, the dish has a positive squeeze of lemon test.

7. **Beaujolais with Polish sausage and sauerkraut**: This is a good match; the acidity of the wine is greater than or equal to that of the dish.

8. **Cortese de Gavi (tart Italian wine) with shrimp scampi (shrimp with a tomato based sauce)**: Good match. The dish has a positive squeeze of lemon test and the acidity of the wine is greater than that of the dish.

9. **Riesling Kabinett served with grilled chicken topped with a sweet and tart pineapple-lemon relish**: Good match. The dish is sweet and tart and so is the wine. Rieslings have good levels of clean crisp acidity.

10. **Pinot Grigio (Italian) served with grilled chicken topped with tart apple-lemon relish**: Good Match. Pinot Grigio is the Italian version of Pinot Gris. It is lightweight and has good levels of tartness that tie into the dish.

Don't feel discouraged if you answered some of these questions wrong. The quizzes are more of a learning experience than they are testing your knowledge. If you answered most of the questions correctly...Bravo!

CHAPTER 9
Weight

Ahh...big, rich, and full-bodied.

The weight or body of a wine is a very important consideration in matching wine to food. Big heavy, robust wines wallop lighter styled foods. However, big heavy, robust dishes do not intimidate light styled wines. Just as a heavy infusion of oak can obscure the more delicate flavors in a wine, the flavors in big, heavy, full-bodied wines will blot out the delicate flavors in light, elegant dishes. **Big, full-bodied wines should only be paired to, rich, heavyweight dishes.**

A heavy wine will be high in alcohol and full-bodied; most will also have a healthy bevy of concentrated flavors. Oak aging will also add to the weight of a wine. Red wines generally have a fuller body than white wines; however, the white Rhônes and some of the richer and fuller Chardonnays can have more weight than some of the lighter reds.

The majority of lighter weight wines have good crisp acidity. Such wines can be paired with a variety of foods—both light and heavy. The tartness and bright flavors in these wine serve to support and season the foods they accompany.

In spite of the fact that lightweight wines have universal acceptance and can be paired with any food regardless of weight, **it is always best to match the weight of a wine to that of the food it accompanies**. Matching weight for weight is yet another way to create harmony in your wine food marriages. I know what you're thinking—I have just contradicted myself! Let me clarify. It is often not possible to pair every facet of a wine's character to that of the accompanying food. If you can match more characteristics between wine and food with a particular lightweight wine, you may have to forgo the linkage in regard to weight. As you read on, you will find that in some cases, lightweight wines will be the best choice for certain heavyweight dishes. Heavyweight wines can wallop a lightweight dish, but it is unlikely that lightweight wines will be intimidated by a heavy dish. Be aware that there are exceptions. Certain very highly seasoned heavyweight foods, such as pepper steak, can blot out the flavors of some of the more delicate wines. Nevertheless, this is the exception, not the rule.

It would be a mistake to serve a big, full-bodied wine, such as a rich, low acid, oaky Australian Chardonnay, with a light dish, such as poached filet of sole. The wine would hammer the dish. However, a lightweight German Riesling Kabinett will pair-up very favorable with a rich dish, such as roast duck topped with a sweet-tart orange sauce. The tartness and sweet flavors in the Riesling tie beautifully into the dish.

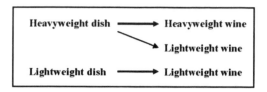

Figure 17 Lightweight wines and heavy weight wines are compatible with heavy weight dishes. Nevertheless if is always preferable to match the weight of the wine with that of the dish. Lightweight foods are only compatible with lightweight wines.

Rich, full-bodied, and flavorful wines have limitations in wine-food marriages, because they can only be paired to big, rich dishes that share similar characteristics. For this reason, you will find light to medium-bodied wines to be more versatile in matching with foods. Unfortunately, there is often a paucity of such wines on the wine lists in many restaurants.

Because the mind seeks harmony in wine-food parings, one should make an attempt to match the weight of wine with the weight of the food they accompany. It is one of the important facets by which you can tie a wine with food. Such parallel connections create symmetry. Symmetry creates harmony, and harmony creates pleasure. You don't have to be exact in matching weight for weight, but shy away from the extremes. For example, don't match a heavyweight wine with a lightweight dish. However, a medium weight wine will work very well with a light-medium weight dish as well as a medium-heavy dish. Although you can be lax in serving lightweight wines to heavier weight dishes, you should be persnickety about serving heavier wines to lighter dishes.

Weights of Foods

Sauces make a big contribution to the weight of a particular food item. Poached chicken breast topped with a vinaigrette sauce will be decidedly lighter than the same breast topped with rich creamy gravy.

Temperature also has an important influence on the weight of a dish. Roast of beef served cold will be decidedly lighter than the same the dish served hot. Fats that are in a solid state are lighter than melted fats. **Cold temperatures suppress flavors and lessen the weight of a food.**

The weight of a food product can differ drastically depending on the mode of its preparation: cold lobster meat over lettuce is light-bodied while lobster Newberg, a hot dish topped with a sauce made of butter, cream, and egg yolk, is very full-bodied: cold temperatures lighten dishes, and rich sauces make them heavy.

The type of cooking method is another significant factor in determining weight. For example, poached chicken will be considerably lighter than blackened chicken. Obviously, fatty cuts of meat will be richer and heavier than leaner cuts: a filet of beef will be lighter than prime rib.

Intensity of flavor and the weight (or body) of a food are closely associated. A good portion of the flavors in a food product is bound to its fat content. A filet of beef has lower fat and lower flavors then a New York strip. Fat in food serves a function similar to alcohol in wine: both are dominant contributors to weight.

Low fat items (fish, chicken, veal) are lighter and more delicately flavored than fatty foods (prime rib, lamb chops, duck). The exception to this pattern is game, which is often very lean, but also very flavorful. The great intensity of flavor in game is the reason that it can tolerate rich, full-flavored wines.

When game is prepared, its weight is also invariably jacked up by larding, wrapping with bacon, basting with fats, or by serving them with rich, full-bodied gravies. These methods of preparation compounded to game's rich, full flavors make game great partners for powerful, full-bodied wines. However, be careful of domestically raised game; they have considerably less flavor than game from the wild. Even wild game's flavor is variable; for example, deer that poach corn from a nearby farm will be less flavorful and less gamy than those who eat from the wild.

The chart below outlines the relative weight of foods and delineates how they change depending on preparation.

Weight of Food					
Food	*Temp.*	*Tartness*	*Sauce*	*Preparation*	**Weight**
Fish				Uncooked	
Shellfish	Cold	Tart	Light-weight (Vinaigrette)	Steaming	**Light**
Meaty fish				Poaching	
Chicken	↓	↓	↓	Sautéing	
Turkey				Frying	
Veal	Warm	Neutral	Medium Wt.	Roasting	
Pork				Broiling	
Beef	↓	↓	↓	Grilling	
Lamb				Braising	
Duck	Hot	Sweet	Heavy-weight (Rich, thick, creamy)	Smoking	**Heavy**
Game				Blackening	

Figure 18

The arrow in the shaded column on the right side of the graph directs the transformation from lightweight foods to heavyweights. In all of the categories above, weight increases as you progress from top to bottom. The weight of foods spans through a large spectrum of categories. Note how temperature, tartness, sauces, and method of preparation affect the weight of a food.

Weights of Wines

The relative weights of wines are outlined in the chart below. Obviously, wine styles can vary. There are big heavy Port styled Zinfandels and there are also lighter styled white Zinfandels. The wines listed below represent the varietal in its most typical style. This chart is not meant to be exact, but it will give you a general idea of the relative weights of wines.

Relative Weights of Wines		
White	Weight	*Red*
Champagne		
White Italian		
Riesling		
Sancerre	Light	
Pouilly Fumé		
Chablis		
Sauvignon Blanc		
White Burgundy		Bardolino
Calif. Chardonnay		Valpolicella
White Rhônes		Beaujolais
		Chianti
		Oregon Pinot Noir
		Calif. Pinot Noir
		Red Burgundy
		Bordeaux
		Cabernet Sauvignon
	Heavy	Syrah
		Zinfandel
		Barolo

Figure 19 A schematic representation of the relative weights of wines. Wines progressively increase in weight from top to bottom.

As you can see, there is a crossover in the relative weights of wines, but most white wines are lighter than red wines. At the crossover point you can see that, in this scheme, white Rhône is heavier than Bardolino.

Too Much of a Good Thing

There is a caveat in matching a heavy wine to a heavy rich food. The combination of a big, soft, round, rich, wine, low in acids and tannins—called **fat wines**— with rich, hefty, full-bodied dishes can be cloying—too much weight! Foods rich in fats and starches can be ponderous by themselves and serving them with a fat wine will only increase the burden.

> ## Fat Wine + Fat Food = Cloying Sensation

Figure 20

Serve fat wines with soft, round dishes that have a sensation of lightness. A thin, light, creamy sauce will have a sense of lightness: however, that same sauce thickened with cheese or roux can become ponderous. The combination of rich cream sauce with starchy foods such as mashed potatoes or pasta further increases the feeling of heaviness.

Big, heavy, rich, foods plus soft, rich, round, full-bodied wines are a sure formula for heartburn and that uncomfortable bloated feeling—bring on the Alka Seltzer! Serve rich, heavy foods with rich wines high in acids or tannins. Remember, acids and tannins decrease weight and richness in wines; they do the same to foods.

Acids have a rapier quality that cuts through richness, and tannins react with fats and proteins to aid in their digestion. A food product in and of itself will similarly be lightened if it is pickled or served with a tart sauce.

Weight for Weight

The following are some examples of successful wine-food combinations:

1. Champagne with sushi—a light wine and food

2. Dry Riesling with boiled Lobster—a light wine and food

3. Riesling Kabinett with Oriental lemon chicken—a light wine and food

4. Pinot Noir with grilled shark steak—a moderate weight wine and foods

5. Chianti with grilled chicken tenders—a moderate weight wine and food

6. Cabernet Sauvignon with lamb chops—a heavy weight wine and food

7. Zinfandel with meatloaf, mashed potatoes and gravy—a heavy weight wine and food

8. Beef Wellington (tenderloin stuffed with foie gras, topped with mushrooms, and wrapped in puffed pastery) with mature red Bordeaux—a moderate-heavy weight wine and food

Quiz

Which of the following would you consider to be successful wine food match-ups? Describe the weight of the wine and food.

1. Chablis with Alaskan king crab and melted butter

2. Sancerre with sautéed herb crusted and breaded calamari steak

3. Barbaresco with fried oysters

4. Riesling Kabinett with sauerbraten (pickled pot roast topped with a mildly sweet ginger flavored gravy), and potato dumplings

5. Beaujolais with fried chicken

6. Viognier with Fettuccini Alfredo (pasta in a rich creamy sauce)

7. Zinfandel with shrimp tempura

Answers

1. **Chablis with Alaskan king crab/melted butter:** This is a light-moderate weight wine with a light-moderate weight dish. In addition, the crisp acidity typically found in Chablis will bolster the flavors in the dish—positive squeeze of lemon test.

2. **Sancerre with sautéed breaded calamari steak:** This is the same scenario as #1. This is a light-moderate weight wine with a light-moderate weight dish. The sautéing somewhat increases the weight of this lightweight food product. The dish has a positive squeeze of lemon test, which further ties the wine to the food.

3. **Barbaresco with fried oysters:** What a disaster. The massive weight of this wine and its rich flavor and high tannin content would pound this light-moderate weight dish to pieces. The delicate flavors in the dish would be completely obliterated.

4. **Riesling Kabinett with sauerbraten with dumplings:** Sauerbraten is pickled beef cooked as a pot roast and served with rich, mildly sweetened ginger flavored gravy. Pickling decreases the weight of a food product, but the thick, rich gravy and heavy dumplings characteristically served with the dish more than make up for its decrease in weight through

pickling. Here we have a lightweight wine paired to a heavy weight dish. Because the dish has tartness, you need a tart wine to pair with it, plus you need acids to cut richness. Riesling has the tartness, and the sweetness in the wine ties into the sweetness of the dish. The ginger flavor in the gravy also associates favorably with the fruity flavors in the wine. Another parallelism of this match-up is ethnicity. This is a German dish that pairs exceedingly well to a German wine.

As lightweight wines have universal acceptance with foods, Riesling makes a good choice. It is interesting to note that in this wine-food combination, we are matching a lightweight white wine to a red meat. This breaks one of the old classic conventions in wine-food pairing—"red wine with red meat."

5. **Beaujolais and fried chicken**: Both the food and the wine are moderate weight, and they both have a note of informality. This is a very good match. Fresh, clean, fruity acidity perks up the flavors in the dish. Here we are matching an informal, moderate weight dish to an informal moderate weight wine.

6. **Viognier with Fettuccini Alfredo**: This is a poor wine-food pairing. A soft, rich, full-bodied wine is paired to a soft, rich, full-bodied dish. So far this sounds pretty good; however, the combination of fat wine with fat dish is cloying—too much weight. The wine-food combination becomes ponderously heavy. To cut its richness, serve Fettuccini Alfredo with a wine that has a good dose of acids or tannins. How about a high quality dry sparkling Italian wine: we have both creamy and tart in the wine. The tart cuts richness and the creamy texture reflects back to the creaminess of the dish.

7. **Zinfandel with shrimp tempura**: What a disaster. The massive weight of this wine and its high tannin content would completely dominate and obliterate this light-moderate weight dish. The delicate flavors in the dish would be decimated.

CHAPTER 10
Flavors

A palette of flavors for the palate!

This chapter deals with integrating the flavors of a wine to its accompanying dish. By tying wine and food flavors together, we refine our pairing by creating parallelism between wine and food. Keep in mind that **the whole idea in making wine-food pairings is to connect similar aspects in the wine to those of the accompanying dish**.

Fruity Flavors

Red and white wines have different flavor profiles. Red wines have flavors of red fruits such as cherries, raspberries, strawberries, plums, and cranberries. White wines have flavors of lighter fleshed fruits such as apples, lemons, grapefruit, pears, apricots, melons, and peaches. The chart below demonstrates the differences in the flavors between red and white wines as well as those flavors common to both.

FRUIT FLAVOR PROFILE FOR WINES		
RED	BOTH	WHITE
Blackberries	Earth	Butter
Raspberries	Herbs	Apples
Strawberries	Flowers	Apricots
Black currants	Nuts	Citrus
Cranberries	Minerals	Figs
Mulberries	Coffee	Lychee
Plumbs	Oak	Melon
Prunes	Oranges	Peaches
Black Cherries	Smoke	Pears
Red Cherries	Spice	Tropical fruits
	Licorice	

Figure 21 Red wines have flavors of red or dark colored fruits; white wines have flavors of lighter colored fruits.

Other Flavors

In addition to fruity flavors, wines have a wide array of food-friendly, non-fruity flavors. In the paragraphs below, you will see how we can use these flavors in matching wine to food. The chart below lists some of the flavors that are found in the more commonly used wines.

NON-FRUIT FLAVORS IN WINE	
Cabernet Sauvignon	Spices, herbs, earth, bell peppers, chocolate, mushrooms, truffles, coffee minerals, flowers
Pinot Noir	Beets, smoke, meat, spices and herbs
Merlot	Chocolate, minerals
Syrah	Hickory smoked grilled game, seared meats, pepper, cinnamon, cloves, licorice, pine
Sangiovese	Smoke, spice, nuts
Nebbiolo	Earth, smoke, coffee
Zinfandel	Black pepper & other spices, herbs, chocolate
Chardonnay	Butter, nuts, smoke, butterscotch
Gewürztraminer	Rose petals, fried bacon, spices
Sauvignon Blanc	Green vegetables (beans, asparagus, peppers, flint, earth

Figure 22 Non-fruity flavors in wine

In this chapter, we refine our wine-food parings by interacting the flavors in wine with those in food. Favorable combinations of these flavors create a sense of harmony, which in turn produces pleasure. The enjoyment that you derive by combining the correct wine with food is synergistic—the effect is greater than the sum of its parts. That is, the enjoyment of a wine successfully married to a food is greater than the pleasure derived from the wine alone plus the enjoyment of the food alone.

The fruity flavor profiles for red and white wines are fairly consistent, but there are some crossovers. For example, black currants, a red wine fruit flavor, is common in Sauvignon Blanc, and orange flavors, which are more common in white wines, can also be found in red wines. However, these exceptions are uncommon.

Over the centuries, chefs have found that certain food combinations complement each other: turkey and cranberries, apples and pork, lobster and butter, fish and lemons, mint and lamb, chicken and curry, and there are many more. As you will see, these classic combinations are a great aid in helping us determine favorable wine-food pairings.

In pairing wine flavors to food, you can either **reflect** the flavors of a wine to the food, or you can **complement** the flavors in food by specific flavors in a wine.

Reflecting Flavors

Consider the classical combination of roast pork and fried apples. When pork is served with apples, you can reflect the specific flavor of apples found in certain wines to the fried apples served with pork. This serves to tie the wine to the food. It creates symmetry: apple flavor in food product reflects to apple flavor in wine. Since apples are a white wine flavor, a white wine would be appropriate for this dish. If the white wine that you choose is devoid of apple flavors, don't worry, as white wine flavors blend wonderfully with each other and will likewise blend splendidly to the flavors of the pork. With such a pairing, you have made a base hit. Nonetheless, always try to be as specific as you can. If you can find a wine that does have apple flavors, you have scored a home run.

Try to tailor your wine-food match as precisely as you can. Sometimes it is not fruit that you are considering, but other items on the plate. For example, if the pork was served with mashed potatoes and asparagus spears, you might select a Sauvignon Blanc. The green vegetal flavors found in Sauvignon Blanc reflect wonderfully to the asparagus (green flavors) in the dish.

Even visual elements can serve as points to reflect a wine's flavor. For example, Indian sweets, such as *ras gulas, gulab jamun,* and *biriani* are commonly flavored with rose water. A clever chef might decorate such dishes with rose petals. Gewürztraminer is a wine that has flavors and scents of rose petals. The visual effect and the scent coming from the dish would make a great focal point to reflect to the floral scent and flavor in the wine.

Complementing Flavors

Now lets consider the situation where pork is served without apples. We now have no specific flavor to reflect to the wine. However, we know that apple flavors are complementary to pork—apples and pork are a classical combination. We can supply that complement by serving pork with a wine that has an apple flavor. A white wine would therefore be appropriate. Again, if the white wine that you choose is devoid of apple flavors, don't worry, as white wine flavors blend wonderfully with each other and will likewise blend favorably to the flavors of the pork. However, try to be as specific in your match as you can.

You will find that a majority of dishes can be created to contain elements containing white wine flavors or red wine flavors. For example, pork can be stuffed with prunes, a red wine flavor, or pork can be served with fried apples, a white wine flavor. The fact that both flavors blend with pork indicates that pork is a versatile meat that can be complemented by either red or white wines. If the pork was served with neutral accompanying items devoid of fruit, such as pork cutlets, mashed potatoes, and carrots, you could choose either a red or a white wine.

As you can see, to make a successful wine-food pairing, you must consider more than just the primary food item. You must look at the accompanying items: gravy, stuffing, relishes, condiments, vegetables or any other items on the plate.

Quiz

Select the wines that best fit the dish. More than one wine may be selected. Indicate your first choice. When you do this exercise, look up the wine's profiles and pick the wine that best matches the dish.

---

1. **Pan-fried filet of sole with an herb infused lemon butter sauce, wild rice, and green peas:** (a) Bardolino—a light Italian red, (b) Sancerre—a wine made from Sauvignon Blanc grapes, (c) Australian Chardonnay, (d) Pinot Noir

2. **Grilled tuna steak with a mild red cherry barbecue sauce, potato cakes, sliced red beets**: (a) Cabernet Sauvignon, (b) Pinot Noir, (c) white Châteauneuf du Pape, (d) California Chardonnay

3. **Pork loin stuffed with goat cheese and spinach, mashed potatoes, buttered carrots and asparagus:** (a) Sauvignon Blanc, (b) Zinfandel, (c) Barolo—an Italian wine made from the Nebbiolo grape, (d) Hermitage—a Syrah from the Rhône Valley

4. **Grilled Salmon topped with an unsweetened cranberry relish, and mashed potatoes:** (a) Cabernet Sauvignon, (b) Pinot Noir, (c) Chardonnay, (d) Syrah

5. **Pepper steak (beef) with pan-fried noodles and green beans**: (a) Viognier, (b) red Zinfandel, (c) Red Bordeaux, (d) Chablis—a white Burgundy

6. **Curried shrimp topped with a sweetened curry sauce and garnished with fresh pineapple and peaches:** (a) white Hermitage—a robust white wine from the Rhone valley, (b) Riesling Kabinett, (c) California Pinot Noir, (d) Valpolicella—medium weight Italian red.

7. **Italian styled roast loin of pork stuffed with ground smoked Italian sausage, bread crumbs, dried cherries, prunes, pine nuts, and seasoned with rosemary and coarsely ground black pepper. This is served with Parmesan cheese risotto (rice), and green beans:** (a) California Chardonnay (b) mature Chianti—an Italian wine made predominantly from the Sangiovese grape, (c) Australian Syrah, (d) Cortese di Gavi—a white Italian wine

8. **Filet of Sole crusted with almonds and lemon zest, wild rice, green beans:** (a) Oregon Pinot Noir, (b) Soave, (c) Alsatian Pinot Gris, (d) Alsatian Riesling

Answers

1. **Pan-fried crusted filet of sole with a lemon butter sauce, wild rice, and green peas:** The best choice is (b): Sancerre. The weight of the wine and food match and the citrus and herb flavors in the wine match those of the food, in addition, the tartness of the wine serves to bolster the flavors in the dish (positive squeeze of lemon test).

2. **Grilled tuna steak with red cherry barbecue sauce, potato cakes, sliced red beets and butter:** (b): Pinot Noir would be the best choice. The red fruit flavors in the barbecue sauce tie to the flavors in the wine, and both the wine and the food are of medium weight. The flavors of beets also reflect beautifully to similar flavors in the wine. Cabernet Sauvignon is too heavy and too tannic for this dish.

3. **Pork loin stuffed with goat cheese and spinach, mashed potatoes, buttered carrots and asparagus: (a) Sauvignon Blanc:** This wine will tie into the green flavors in the asparagus and spinach. Goat cheese also has a natural affinity to Sauvignon Blanc (more about this later). All of the other wines are too heavy.

4. **Grilled Salmon topped with an unsweetened cranberry relish, carrots, and mashed potatoes.** (b) Pinot Noir: All of the other wines are full-bodied and too heavy for this dish. The Pinot Noir is medium weight and as is the dish, Flavors of cranberry also reflect to the red wine flavors in Pinot Noir.

5. **Pepper steak (beef) with pan-fried noodles and green beans:** (b): Zinfandel is a very good choice. The peppery flavors in the dish tie to the black pepper flavors and the briary notes so common in the wine. Both food and wine are full-bodied, and both wine and food are aggressive. Bordeaux is too sophisticated and is out of character for this dish. Viognier and Chablis would be overpowered; their delicate flavors would be clobbered. This is the uncommon situation where the food intimidates the wine.

6. **Curried shrimp topped with a sweetened curry sauce and garnished with fresh pineapple and peaches:** (b): Riesling Kabinett: The white fruit flavors and sweetness reflect to similar savors in the dish. This dish also has a positive squeeze of lemon test, and Riesling is a tart and sweet wine. Hermitage is too heavy. Valpolicella and Pinot Noir have red fruit flavors that don't fit the context of the dish.

7. **Italian styled roast loin of pork stuffed with ground smoked Italian sausage, dried cherries, prunes, and pine nuts, seasoned with rosemary and coarsely grounded black pepper. This is served with Parmesan cheese risotto (rice), and green beans:** (a) and (b): Chianti is the best choice. Flavors of cherries, prunes, nuts, spice, and smoke, in both of these wines reflect to similar flavors in this dish. Both the dish and the wine are moderate weight and Italian. Here we have tied the wine to the flavors in the dish, its Italian ethnicity, and its weight. The Syrah is perhaps a little too heavy; besides, it's not Italian. Cortese is a white wine whose flavors do not reflect to the dish.

8. **Filet of Sole crusted with almonds and lemon zest, wild rice, green beans:** (b): Soave is a good match. The flavors of almonds and lemons in Soave reflect into this dish. The dish is light bodied and so is the wine. The dish also has a positive squeeze of lemon test, and Soave is a high-acid wine. Pinot Noir is a bit too big and has red wine flavors that do not reflect into the dish. The Pinot Gris has only moderate acid levels and is a little hefty for the dish. The Alsatian Riesling has good acidity, but is too full-bodied.

CHAPTER 11
Umami

Umami, the newly discovered fifth taste sensation, is found in a wide variety of foods. Indeed, umami can be found in a number of mature wines. For many years it has been accepted as a taste sensation in Asian cuisines, but its acceptance is new to the Western World.

An exact description of umami is difficult to formulate. There is somewhat of a mystical or spiritual element to this elusive, metaphysical fifth taste sensation. It is a much more difficult taste sensation to understand as compared to the classical four: sweet, tart, bitter, and salt. Foods with high levels of umami have a sense of perfection: a food flawlessly prepared from high quality or fully ripened ingredients. Some of the adjectives used to describe umami include savory, succulent, delicious, rich and ripe, and meaty. However, these terms fall somewhat short of the full meaning of the word. The best way to get a handle on this term is to taste it. Place a tiny dab of monosodium glutamate (MSG) on the tip of your tongue: I'll let you come up with your own description. I find it to have a slightly sweet and salty taste reminiscent of grilled meats and mushrooms. One of the surprising characteristics of this taste sensation is its marvelously prolonged aftertaste. The taste sensation lingers for several minutes after sampling. Just as in wine, the longer the aftertaste, the more enjoyable the sensation will be. A prolonged and pleasant aftertaste is a hallmark sign of quality in both wine and food.

Umami is produced by stimulating special taste receptor cells with specific amino acids. A team of scientists from the University of Miami has positively identified these taste receptor cells. The discovery of these receptor sites fully legitimizes umami as a fifth taste sensation. Glutamates (as in MSG) have the strongest stimulatory effect; however other amino acids such as aspartates can also elicit the sensation.

Umami in Foods

Nature abounds with foods rich in umami. The chart below lists some of the more common foods that have high levels of umami. As you can see from the chart below, Asian foods will generally be loaded with umami producing ingredients.

Umami can be increased in foods in a number of ways. **Braising and stewing** can increase umami in meats: pot roast has more umami than pan-fried beef. **Curing** can also increase the umami content in foods: corned beef has more umami than steak. **Processing** can increase the sensory appreciation of umami: tomato paste, tomato juice, and sun-dried tomatoes all have more umami than fresh tomatoes. **Aging** meats has a significant effect as well: a well-aged piece of beef will have more umami than freshly killed meats. **Smoking** foods also is an efficient method to increase umami in a food product: smoked ham and bacon have more umami than pork chops. **Broths** concentrate the umami content from the products from which they are made: bullion and consommés are prime examples.

UMAMI	
Umami rich foods	**Umami produced byTreatment**
Kelp	Cured meats (brisket etc.)
Seaweed	Braised or stewed meats (beef, chicken)
Bonito	Dried foods (sardines, tomatoes, mushrooms etc.)
Green tea	Processed foods (tomato paste, tomato juice)
Cheese	Broth (bullion, dashi, consommés)
Sardine	Aging (aging increases umami in beef)
Mushrooms	Smoking (ham, bacon etc)
Tomatoes-dried	
Tomatoes-fully ripe	
Oysters	
Sardines	
Mackerel	
Tuna	

Figure 23 Foods listed on the left column are unusually high in umami. In the right column are listed various methods of preparation of a food product that will increase the umami content of the natural food.

Wine-Food Interactions

Not all wines will develop umami. However, you will find umami in some high quality, perfectly matured wines. These wines will have a multidimensional quality: a layering of ripe, savory flavors that hang-on to produce a long, lingering, and savory aftertaste.

Wines with umami can react with foods to produce a wide range of synergistic responses. Such wine-food combinations represent the epitome of high cuisine. This is a prime reason that fully matured wines are served with savory dishes. These wines need not be shockingly expensive, and are made in wineries worldwide.

The Clash of the Titans

Tannins in red wines and oak in white wines can have major effects on the character of the wine, and each of these elements reacts with umami in a very predictable manner. Wines develop umami when fully matured. At this point in their development, tannins have softened and flavors have peaked. This is fortunate because tannins clash with umami. **When tannic wines are served with foods high in umami, the tannins are accentuated and they develop a bitter, metallic taste.** If you are looking for a red wine to match with a food high in umami, select wines that are characteristically low in tannins, such Pinot Noir or mature wines whose tannins have had a chance to mellow.

In similar fashion, **oaky white wines** react with foods high in umami in a derogatory fashion. The umami in foods increases the oaky character of the wine making the wine ponderously rich and full-bodied. If you are looking for a white wine to serve with a food high in umami, a crisp, light to medium bodied unoaked wine will usually be the best choice.

Quiz

Which of the following would be considered favorable wine-food combinations.

1. Youthful Barolo with beef stewed together with mushrooms, tomato paste, beef broth, and onions

2. Chablis with oysters

3. Fruity flavored ham with a German Riesling

4. Filet mignon stuffed with oysters and mushrooms and cheese served with a young aggressive Cabernet Sauvignon

5. Fully matured, high quality Morey-St. Denis (red Burgundy) served with Beef Bourguignonne (beef braised in Burgundy wine garnished with white onions and mushrooms)

6. Oaky Australian Chardonnay served with a chicken roulade (thin slice of meat rolled around a filling) stuffed with cheese, ham, mushrooms and breadcrumbs

7. Champagne with sushi

8. Young Hermitage (red Rhône) with chicken cacciatore (braised chicken with tomatoes, tomato paste, mushrooms and onions)

9. Tuna with a mushroom gravy served with a fully matured, premium Pinot Noir

10. Mature high quality Chianti with spaghetti topped with a sun-dried tomato sauce

Answers

1. **Youthful Barolo with beef stewed together with mushrooms, tomato paste, beef broth, and onions:** This is a poor combination. This dish is loaded with umami producing ingredients: mushrooms, tomato paste, and beef bullion. In addition the beef is stewed, which will increase its umami content. The high tannins in this youthful Barolo will clash with the high umami content of this dish.

2. **Chablis with oysters:** This is a classic combination of a dry, unoaked wine with a dish high in umami.

3. **Fruity flavored ham with a German Riesling**: This is a great combination of a fruity, unoaked wine with a fruity dish high in umami.

4. **Filet mignon stuffed with oysters and mushrooms and cheese served with young aggressive Cabernet Sauvignon**: Although steak and Cabernet Sauvignon make a good combination, the addition of cheese and mushrooms, foods high in umami, totally change the character of this dish. The high tannins in a young Cabernet would likely clash with the umami in this dish.

5. **Fully matured, high quality Morey-St. Denis (red Burgundy) served with Beef Bourguignonne (beef braised in Burgundy wine garnished with white onions and mushrooms):** This is a classic combination. The spectrum of synergies created between a wine that is likely high in umami served with a dish with obvious umami (braised beef and mushrooms) will be a marvel.

6. **Oaky Australian Chardonnay served with a chicken roulade (thin slice of meat rolled around a filling) stuffed with cheese, ham, mushrooms and breadcrumbs:** A poor combination. Oaky wines clash with foods high in umami.

7. **Champagne with sushi:** This is a classic combination of a dry, unoaked sparkling wine combined with a dish high in umami.

8. **Young Barbaresco with chicken cacciatore (braised chicken with tomatoes, tomato paste, mushrooms and onions):** Poor wine food pairing. This is a classical example of a dish high in umami clashing with a wine high in tannin.

9. **Tuna with a mushroom gravy served with a fully matured, premium Pinot Noir:** This is a marvelous synergetic union. Here we have a dish high in umami paired to a wine low in tannin and possibly high in umami.

10. **Mature high quality Chianti with spaghetti topped with a sun-dried tomato sauce.** This is another synergetic union.

Here we have a dish high in umami (sun dried tomatoes) paired to a wine low in tannin (mature wine) and possibly high in umami.

CHAPTER 12
Sweet and Spicy Hot Foods

"I'll have five bird's nests, one shark fin, a dozen 100-year-old eggs, two bottles five spice powder, and one carton of cigarettes."

Spicy Hot Foods

It is interesting to note that Asia has traditionally favored the notion of 6 basic tastes: sweet, sour, salty, bitter, umami, and hot (like in Tabasco). However, the sensation of "hot" has not been accepted as a "taste" by the culinary establishment in this country.

The spicy heat found in many ethnic dishes is a somewhat difficult element to contend with in wine-food pairings. If it is too powerful, forget about wine, you are better off with beer. There are no wines that can stand up to the intense heat in some of the more extreme Indian, Thai, or Mexican dishes.

Moderate spicy-hot dishes can easily be paired to wines. The spicy heat in such foods can be assuaged by sweetness in the accompanying wine. **Sweetness tames the aggressiveness of spicy heat,** yet you are still able to enjoy the spicy-hot kick from the food. That doesn't mean that dry wines will not work, but if you use them, stick with light to medium bodied wines. Choose the wines as you would with any other food; mild to moderate spicy heat will usually not affect the character of the wine or its ability to pair-up with food. Nonetheless, sweet wines have a definite advantage. Oriental foods with spicy heat are often great matches for sweet wines.

Another problem with spicy-hot foods is that they will accentuate the heat derived from alcohol in wine. A wine might have high, but very tolerant alcohol levels that do not induce the sensation of alcoholic heat. However, when paired with a spicy hot dish, that same wine may well develop the pugnacious bite of high alcohol. A synergy is formed between the alcoholic heat in the wine and the spicy heat in the dish, which can make the combination unpleasant. **Do not serve high alcohol wines with spicy hot dishes.**

Sweet Foods

Sweet is a very powerful taste sensation. A sweet dish begs to find some sweetness in the accompanying wine. Sweetness in wine reflects to the sweetness in the dish, which creates symmetry and ties the wine to the food.

The mind subconsciously compares the sweetness of the wine against the sweetness of the food. If the food is sweeter than the wine, the acidity of the wine will be accented. The wine will taste lighter and tarter than it actually is, making it appear out of balance. The food will wreck the wine! **Always keep the sweetness of wine equal to or greater than the sweetness of the dish**. This effect is especially noticeable in dessert wines. Super sweet deserts are difficult to pair to wines because it is difficult to find a wine with sufficient sweetness to stand up to the food.

Foods accompanied by sweet items such as relishes, sauces, dressings, jellies, or sweet condiments of any type are prime candidates for sweet wines. Such dishes are common on restaurant menus, yet only a few restaurants will offer a wine with sufficient sweetness to pair-up to the food—in fact, in most restaurants, sweet wines are frowned upon. However, California or Australian Chardonnay, an often-poor wine to pair with a majority of dishes, can be found on restaurant wine lists in abundance. Chardonnay is a name the public knows and accepts as a wine for all occasions, when in fact it is not.

Care must be exercised when overtly sweet foods are served with dry wines. For example, when duck topped with a sweet orange glaze is served with a dry wine, the sweetness in the dish could very well intimidate the wine, and balance will appear disrupted. However, if sweetness is mild, wine's ripe fruity flavors and the sweetness derived from its alcohol will usually suffice to keep the wine in balance. In foods with mild natural sweetness, such as corn, peas, winter squash, and the like, there is usually enough sweetness derived from the alcohol in a dry wine to reflect into the food; however, wines with a little residual sugar will also make a good fit.

Very sweet wines such as Riesling Auslese or Beerenauslese are often too sweet for most dishes that are devoid of sweetness. However, very rich dishes can sometimes accommodate a wine with high residual sugars: foie gras and Sauternes, Roquefort cheese and Bonnezeaux, and Stilton cheese and Port are classic examples. Sweetness in wine engenders a feeling of excess that pairs up to rich dishes. It both brightens and reinforces the flavors of the dish. However, in most cases of non-dessert dishes, you will be more successful if you limit your selection of wines to sweetness comparable to Riesling Kabinett or Spätlese.

Sweetness is a very powerful taste sensation that tends to carry over to subsequent courses. Such courses are, therefore, best saved for the end of the meal. If this is not possible, a short starchy course following the sweet course will help to readjust the palate.

Spicy Hot and Sweet Foods

Many dishes are both spicy hot and sweet. In these instances, the sweetness in the wine serves a dual purpose. It reflects itself into the sweetness of the dish while at the same time mitigates the spicy heat. Many of the dishes that contrast sweet against tart are of ethnic origin, especially from the Orient. It is unfortunate that many Oriental restaurants do not serve wine. The most likely reason that wines are not offered with Oriental cuisine is that it is not the custom of their country to drink wine. A great number of Oriental restaurants have no wine list at all, and if they do, the list might not contain a single sweet wine. However, with the growing interest in wine, the trend is changing.

A great choice for spicy hot and sweet dishes is a sweet styled Riesling. It has a wide range of sweetness, it's low in alcohol, it's light-bodied, and it has good crisp acidity. German Rieslings are quality wines at an affordable price. However, if the heat is high, the flavors in the wine have a tendency to flag. Rieslings work very well with most Chinese dishes, but in some spicy hot Thai or Indian dishes, the heat is simply too much. Drink beer.

Other choices for readily available sweet wines include sweeter styled Chenin Blanc wines, such as Vouvray; Sauvignon Blanc with a degree of residual sugars; or German and California Gewurztraminer.

Quiz

Select the best wine for the food.

---

1. **Sweet and sour pork (with pineapple, green peppers and onions):** (a) Riesling Kabinett, (b) Sweet styled Sauvignon Blanc, (c) Alsatian Gewürztraminer, (d) Viognier

2. **Duck with a sweet orange sauce:** (a) Pinot Noir, (b) sweet styled Pinot Gris, (c) young red Zinfandel, (d) young Barolo.

3. **Spicy hot Thai Chicken with lemon grass:** (a) Chardonnay, (b) Beer, (c) Pinot Noir, (d) Riesling Kabinett

4. **Chorizo sausage (moderate spicy hot) in tomato sauce over rice:** (a) dry Gewürztraminer, (b) Chardonnay, (c) Barolo (d) Beaujolais

Answers

1. **Sweet and sour pork** (a) Riesling Kabinett: If you want to emphasize the vegetal component of the dish (green peppers) Sauvignon Blanc would work. However, I always prefer to emphasize the fruity component (pineapple). It is the more pleasurable of the two flavors. Riesling would be a preferred choice. Alsatian Gewürztraminer and Viognier are too heavy; and although Gewürztraminer may have some sweetness, Viognier never does. Because of the exotic flavors in Gewürztraminer, many people tend to lean toward them with exotic Oriental foods. However, Alsatian Gewürztraminer's rich body, low acidity, and high alcohol make it a difficult choice to match with foods.

2. **Duck with a sweet orange sauce:** (b) The only sweet wine is the Pinot Gris; it's the obvious choice. In addition, the orange flavor commonly found in the wine reflects beautifully to the dish.

3. **Spicy hot Thai chicken with lemon grass:** (b), (d), If there is too much heat; go with beer. With moderate heat, The Riesling Kabinett is a great choice.

4. **Spicy chorizo sausage in tomato sauce over rice:** (d) Beaujolais has good tart acidity to stand up to the tomato sauce and moderate alcohol that will not be accentuated by the heat from the chorizo sausage. The ripe fruity flavors in the wine also give is a sense of sweetness that allows the wine to stand up to the spicy heat in the dish. The two whites and the Barolo have high alcohol levels that could produce alcoholic heat. They also do not fit the rustic character of the dish.

CHAPTER 13
Salty Foods

Salt is not a significant ingredient in wine; however, in regard to food, salt is a very important taste sensation. Like acids and sugars, it is a sensation that is very important in the development of flavor. Excesses of salt can ruin a dish, but just the right amount can dramatically increase flavor.

Tannic Wines and Salty Foods

Salt in food interacts with wine in a manner very similar to acidity. Just as acids and tannins are synergistic, so it is with salt and tannin. **The perception of tannins and the bitterness of tannins are increased when paired to salty foods**. Red wines become rougher and less sophisticated—they lose their polish. Because of this effect, most salty foods will work best with white wines, rosé wines, or reds with lower levels of tannins, such as Beaujolais or

Bardolino. However, choose wines with good levels of acidity, as foods high in salt will make low to moderately tart wines appear flat and out of balance.

Sweet Wines and Salty Food

Sweetness counterbalances acidity; it does the same with salt. **Sweet wines react with salty foods in a manner that lessens the perception of saltiness.** The sweetness in a wine balances salty taste and makes salty food taste better. Sweet white wines are abundant, but if a dish calls for a red, you will have more difficulty in making a selection. Sweet red wines are seldom paired with non-dessert items. The best solution is to pick a dry red wine that has abundant ripe fruity flavors, which gives the impression of sweetness. Wines with ripe fruity flavors can taste sweet even though the wine is relatively low in alcohol and contains no residual sugar. The mind subconsciously associates ripe fruit with sweetness.

Tart Wines and Salty Foods

Tart wines taste less acidic when paired to salty foods. This is the same scenario that occurs when you pair an acid wine to an acid food. Salt gives food the vague impression that it has been acidified—a sort of pseudo acidity. If this perceived acidity (actually salt) is greater in the food than it is in the wine, the wine will taste flat and out of balance. The food will corrupt the wine! To compensate for this effect, **wine should have good levels of acidity when paired to salty foods**. Salty foods will make wines with low acidity will appear dull, flat, and flabby. Choose young tart white wines to pair to salty foods.

From the above discussions, we can conclude that **salty foods prefer wines with sweetness and tartness, but low levels of tannins.** Good choices of readily obtainable wines would be sweet versions of Riesling, Vouvray, and Sauvignon Blanc.

There can be a problem in selecting a tart red wine with low levels of tannin, because many quality young tart reds will also have high levels of tannins. However, there are several wines that will work. Less sophisticated wines such as Beaujolais, Chinon, Bardolino, Barbara, or Valpolicella have good levels of acidity, but restrained amounts of tannins. Mature red wines will have lower levels of tannins; however, they will also likely have lower levels of acidity.

Quiz

Choose the best wine to match to the following menu items.

---

1. **Baked ham topped with a sweet pineapple glaze and decorated with cherries, cloves and pineapple chunks:** (a) Soave, (b) Riesling Kabinett, (c) Alsatian Gewürztraminer, (d) California Chardonnay

2. **Prosciutto wrapped melon balls:** (a) Soave, (b) Riesling Kabinett, (c) Viognier, (d) Australian Chardonnay

3. **Pan-fried chicken crusted with herb flavored goat cheese and walnuts, served with asparagus spears and oven roasted potatoes:** (a) mild sweet styled Sauvignon Blanc, (b) Australian Chardonnay, (c) Riesling Kabinett, (d) Cabernet Sauvignon

4. **Corned beef and cabbage, boiled potatoes, parsnips, turnips, and carrots** (a) Soave, (b) Beaujolais, (c) Gewürztraminer, (d) California Chardonnay

5. **Saltimbocca (veal wrapped in Prosciutto, seasoned with sage, and then sautéed):** (a) Barbaresco, (b) Valpolicella, (c) Montepulciano d'Abruzzo, (d) high quality super Tuscan

Answers

1. **Baked ham topped with a sweet pineapple glaze and decorated with cherries, cloves and pineapple chunks**: (b) Riesling: Ham is salt cured meat that has distinctly perceptive saltiness. The sweet pineapple and cherry decorations add additional sweetness and fruitiness. Riesling is a great match; it has sweetness and plenty of acidity. In addition, the fruity flavors in the dish reflect to the fruity flavors in the wine. Soave lacks sweetness and has limited fruit. Gewürztraminer and Chardonnay are usually acid deficient and high in alcohol.

2. **Prosciutto wrapped melon balls**: (b) Riesling: The saltiness of the Prosciutto (Italian salt cured, unsmoked ham) plus fruitiness makes Riesling the best choice. Viognier and Chardonnay have high alcohol and are too big and too acid deficient. Soave lacks sweetness and fruitiness.

3. **Pan-fried chicken crusted with herb flavored goat cheese and walnuts, and served with asparagus spears and oven roasted potatoes**: (a) Sauvignon Blanc has sweetness and a good dose of acidity, which makes it a good partner for the saltiness of goat cheese. Green flavors in the wine match to green flavors in the dish. In addition, Sauvignon Blanc has an affinity to goat cheese. The herbal and green flavors in the wine reflect to similar flavors (asparagus) in the dish. Riesling would also work, but not as well.

4. **Corned beef and cabbage, boiled potatoes, parsnips, turnips, and carrots**: (b) Beaujolais: Corn beef is salt cured, and parsnips, turnips, and carrots have mild sweetness. Beaujolais is a high acid wine whose ripe fruity flavors give a sense of sweetness to the wine. It is tart enough to overcome the saltiness in the food and low in tannins. Remember,

tannins become accentuated by salty foods and clash with umami.

5. Saltimbocca (veal wrapped in Prosciutto, seasoned with sage, and then sautéed): (b) Valpolicella is a light to medium weight wine with good acidity. The weight of both wine and food match, and there is enough acidity to stand up to the salty taste of the dish. The super Tuscan, Barbaresco, and Montepulciano are too big and tannic. Tannins become accentuated by salty foods and will clash with the umami in the dish (Prosciutto—a processed food).

CHAPTER 14
Refinements

At this point you have mastered the essentials of matching wines with foods. The techniques described in this chapter will add a little polish to your skills. The key to any good wine-food paring is linking the wine with the food along as many facets as you can. The following chapters will provide you with additional paths to tie a wine to food.

Tough and chewy!

Texture

Matching wine to the textural qualities of food is yet another mechanism to shore the union of wine to food. Texture is an important characteristic of both wine and food. Food products that are fine, tender, soft, and smooth require mature, sophisticated, and refined wines that have lost their aggressive edge. In like fashion, dishes that are coarse, chewy, chunky, and less cultivated stack up more successfully to wines that are more rustic and have a somewhat rough and aggressive nature. As you can see, the adjectives that describe food are identical to those that describe wine. When you marry a wine to food, the descriptive characteristics of the wine should match those of the food. A pot roast has a coarse, chunky, and less refined texture that would call for a more rustic wine, whereas the tender nature a filet mignon demands a softer and more mature wine of a stature.

As you have already learned, young wines have rougher and more angular qualities than older wines. As wines mature, the aggressive parts (the acids and tannins) decline, and at full maturity wine becomes smooth, soft, and silky. Coarseness and harshness in a young wine give way to roundness and richness at maturity. The whole composition of the wine changes. The callowness of youth transforms to the sophistication and finesse of maturity.

Match chewy, rough, tough, chunky and unrefined foods with coarse and aggressive features to wines with similar characteristics: Chianti, Montepulciano d'Abruzzo, Gattinara, Zinfandel, Italian whites, Chenin Blanc, Sauvignon Blanc or similar type wines. Tender, refined foods need wines with more noble features: mature red wines such as Cabernet Sauvignon, Pinot Noir, Bordeaux, and Burgundy; or sophisticated whites such as Chablis, white Bordeaux, white Burgundy, high quality Sauvignon Blanc, or Riesling QmP. I am not talking about premier wines with a hefty price tag, but good quality, solid wines in the medium price range.

As you would suspect, **creamy foods** will pair up to wines that have a creamy, rich, round mouth feel, such as a soft ripe Chardonnay, Viognier or a mature Merlot—fat wines. However, remember to keep the total weight of the combination in mind. If the food product is heavy, the combination of fat, creamy wine with rich, heavy food product will produce a cloying feeling of excess. In such cases, you will have to forgo the creamy round bond between wine and food, and move to a wine that has good levels of acids and tannins. Don't forget about Champagne. This is a wine both round and creamy, yet tart and flavor supporting. Champagne is a very food friendly wine often forgotten when matching a wine to food.

You will find that a large number of foods will pair better to younger wines in the middle price range. Save high quality, soft, sophisticated, and refined wines for wine tastings or to serve with fine textured elegant dishes. Most people have the tasting sequence backwards. The majority of the dinner parties that I have attended serve the high priced, noble, soft, round, mature wines with dinner, where they must compete with the elements in food, while the younger and less gifted wines are consumed before hand. Great wines do not need the flavors of food to compete with their intricate balance, complex subtleties, and refined structure. The order should be reversed. Food often competes with and covers over the complex and sophisticated framework of high quality mature wines, whereas the aggressiveness of tart younger wines is often beneficial to food. Their acids perk up flavors, and their tannins mitigate excessive richness.

This is not to say that you should serve poor or average quality wines with your meal. Serve good quality wines, but not great wines. To serve a noble wine like Romanée Conti with Beef Burgundy is a waste. You will have missed many of the wine's subtleties. Drink the Romanée Conti by itself, and serve a lesser but good quality Burgundy, such as a Gevrey Chambertin (village wine), with dinner.

Character

The overall character of the dish is an important consideration. Entrees made with lesser cuts of meat that are combined with ingredients such as cabbage, turnips and the like have an air of informality; whereas dishes using prime cuts of meats combined with ingredients such as truffles, morel mushrooms, and foie gras have a ring of formality. Some dishes are unrefined and full of gusto; others are elegant, sophisticated and complex. Match the qualities of the wine to the character of the dish. Zinfandel and Barolo are big and gutsy, Chablis and M-S-R Riesling are light and elegant, and a high quality Burgundy is rich, sophisticated, and complex. You wouldn't serve premium red Bordeaux with grilled hamburger patties. A casual and informal wine such as Beaujolais or Zinfandel is much more appropriate.

Alphonse, pass up the foie gras.

Ambiance

Ambiance is of paramount importance. It is obvious that foods served on paper plates, with plastic utensils, on a picnic table in the back yard will be perceived to be of a lesser stature than exactly the same dish artistically plated, served under candlelight, on a white tablecloth, with fine china, and sterling silver utensils. Foods served at a picnic call for informal wines; fine dining requires fine wines. A grilled breast of chicken served at a picnic might be served with fresh, light and charming reds such as Chinon, Dolcetto, or Beaujolais; however, that same piece of meat at a formal dinner party calls for a wine of greater stature, such as a Domaine Drouhin Pinot Noir from Oregon or a Robert Mondavi Cabernet Sauvignon.

Wines such as, Gattinara, Montepulciano d'Abruzzo, California Chenin Blanc, Côtes-du-Rhône, early maturing Australian Shiraz, and Beaujolais are commonplace wines. They may be good quality wines, but they will never be great. Such wines will have a lax and informal nature and are great matches for picnics, backyard grills, tailgate parties, and other informal occasions.

Plate Presentation

Plate presentation is another key consideration in matching a wine to food. Quality food dumped onto a plate lends a feeling of cafeteria dining. The same food artistically arranged on fine china and topped with richly colored sauces and garnishes will demand a higher quality wine—and a much higher price tag for both wine and food! There is validity in the old adage: "We eat with our eyes." If you are in the restaurant business, a little low cost artistry can turn into big profits. Too many restaurants place all their emphasis on food preparation and little to none on the artistry of plate presentation. Obviously, quality of the food product is the first consideration; if the food is poorly prepared, it has no salvation. However, plate presentation can elevate a dish from ordinary to the level of gourmet dining. And, gourmet dining calls for good quality wines.

Ethnicity

Foods tend to develop around wines indigenous to their own country. Therefore, it makes good sense to couple foods to wines that have the same ethnicity. Ethnic dishes will have qualities that coordinate with their native wines.

The label on a wine bottle has a powerful psychological effect when you match a wine to food. It just seems fitting to drink an Italian wine with pasta rather than a wine such as California Cabernet Sauvignon or Beaujolais. Even if the qualities of a wine fit perfectly with the context of a dish, there's something missing if there is a disparity in the ethnicity of the wine and food.

In countries like Italy, Spain, and France, you can always find an ethnic wine to match to a food; however, in countries like Greece, Germany, Japan, India, and Israel, you may not be so fortunate. If you are looking for a native red wine for a German dish, you are forced to drink a pedestrian wine called Spätburgunder (and inferior strain of Pinot Noir). That is essentially the only red wine that Germany produces. Choosing a wine from another country may be a better option.

In choosing a wine with the same ethnicity as the dish, you will establish yet another linkage between wine and food.

Quiz

Multiple Choice:
Select the wine that makes the best match to the food.

1. **Crown roast of lamb with a cherry, currant, and bread stuffing**: (a) Barbara, (b) Chardonnay, (c) good quality mature Red Bordeaux, (d) Beaujolais

2. **Pot roast with carrots, onions, parsnips, turnips, and potatoes**: (a) mature Côtes du Rhône, (b) high quality mature red Burgundy, (c) high quality California Sauvignon (d) Sancerre

3. **Baked stuffed lobster**: (a) good quality Pinot Noir, (b) good quality white Burgundy, (c) Frascati, an Italian white wine, (d) Zinfandel

4. **Grilled hot dog, catsup, and pickle relish**:(a) Pinot Noir, (b) quality white Burgundy, (c) Cabernet Sauvignon, (d) Beaujolais

5. **Breaded pan fried clams at a beach party**: (a) Sancerre, (b) California Chardonnay, (c) Pinot Noir, (d) Alsatian Riesling

6. **Osso Buco (Italian styled braised veal shanks) with risotto (Italian styled rice):** (a) red Burgundy, (b) mature high quality Chianti, (c) California Cabernet Sauvignon, (d) Alsatian Riesling

7. **Boeuf Bourguignonne (Beef Burgundy—beef braised in red wine and garnished with white onions and mushrooms:** (a) 1994 Lafarge Côte de Beaune Villages, (b) Chambertin— a Grands Crus red Burgundy (c) 1989 Châteaux Talbot, (d) Beaulieu Pinot Noir

Answers:

1. **Crown roast of lamb with a cherry rice stuffing**: (c) Red Bordeaux: This is a choice cut of lamb prepared in a festive manner. The wine and lamb are of equal weight, the red fruit flavors in the dish (cherries and currants) reflect beautifully into the wine, and the high quality of the food product matches to the noble stature of the wine. The texture and character of the wine match that of the dish.

2. **Pot roast with carrots, onions, parsnips, and potatoes**: (a) mature Côtes du Rhône: This is a very flavorful dish

made from a lesser cut of meat that is braised together with an assortment of vegetables. It's the hearty sort of dish that you might find cooking on a French farmhouse stove. Côtes du Rhône is a hearty, flavorful, French everyday wine that perfectly matches the character and weight of the dish. Because the wine is mature, tannins are low in amount and soft in texture and will not be affected by the high umami content (braised beef) of the dish.

3. **Baked stuffed lobster**: (b) White Burgundy: Lobster, the king of shellfish, deserves a wine of equal stature. White Burgundy is a crisp wine (positive squeeze of lemon test) that matches the weight of the stuffed lobster and gives the dish the stature it deserves.

4. **Grilled hot dog, catsup, and pickle relish**: (d) Beaujolais: This is a very casual dish that fits the informal nature of the wine. Pinot Noir, Cabernet, and white Burgundy are too sophisticated and do not fit the character of the dish.

5. **Breaded pan-fried clams**: (a) Sancerre is the only wine that fits the character of this dish. Both the dish and the wine are of light-moderate weight. Sancerre is a crisp, tart wine that will provide plenty of lemony acidity (positive squeeze of lemon test). Chardonnay, Alsatian Riesling, and Pinot Noir are too big and are out of character with the food. The setting is informal, and so is the wine.

6. **Osso Buco (Italian styled veal shanks) with risotto (Italian styled rice)**: (b) Mature high quality Chianti is a good match for this dish—stay ethnic.

7. **Boeuf Bourguignonne**: (a) 1994 Lafarge Côte de Beaune Villages: This dish is basic French farmhouse cooking. It has a fancy name, but it is nothing more than pot roast. The character of the village wine matches that of the dish. We are also matching an ethnic dish to a wine of the same ethnicity—French. When a dish is made with a certain type of wine, a good rule is to drink the same type of wine with the meal. There is an old saying regarding Boeuf Bourguignonne

that you should braise the beef with one bottle of Chambertin and serve another bottle with the meal. This is ridiculous! Chambertin is an expensive, top quality red Burgundy whose character would be annihilated by the braising process. A sound, inexpensive California Pinot Noir (the grape varietal of Burgundy wine) for a braising liquid would work equally well.

CHAPTER 15
Champagne—the Wine for all Occasions?

Pop—fzzzzzz...

Although this chapter refers to Champagne, any good quality sparkling wine, regardless of the country of origin will be the equal to Champagne in regards to matching wine with food. Good quality sparkling wine is one of the most versatile of all wines. It derives its reputation as a universal wine because of its unique tactile sensation. It is both round and soft, while at the same time it is angular, aggressive, tart, and light. At first hand this seems incongruous. The words aggressive and angular are diametrically opposite to round and soft. The secret of its success lies in the bubbles—the wine's textural quality. The finely beaded mousse of Champagne has a round, soft mouth feel, while the still wine is aggressive, angular, and tart. There is no other wine that will fit this description.

The other dichotomy in Champagne is that many wines that are soft, smooth, and round have high alcohol, which makes them rich and full-bodied. Champagne is a light-bodied wine that, because of its rich creamy mousse, has the quality of being smooth and soft.

The creamy mousse balances the aggressiveness of the still wine; yet, tart, crisp acidity still comes through. Indeed, sparkling wines that lack a quality mousse are tart and rough; the coarse carbonation, coming from big bubbles, actually increases the nettlesome qualities of the wine.

Champagne with Food

Champagne makes a great accompaniment to a wide variety of foods. The creaminess of Champagne combined with its refreshing tartness makes the wine unique in regard to wine-food pairing. Consider creamy based oyster stew; the cream calls for roundness and richness, yet the oysters call for lightness and tartness. Champagne fills the bill to perfection! It is the only wine whose creamy richness will never generate a heavy, cloying sensation of excess no matter the weight of the dish.

In contrast, a soft, round, full-bodied Australian Chardonnay will reflect its smooth, supple, rich character to a full-bodied creamy dish such as Lobster Newberg (lobster in a rich creamy sauce served over toast points). However, the thick, creamy richness of the Newberg sauce combined with a soft full-bodied Chardonnay generates an inordinate amount of weight. This makes the combination cloyingly rich. Australian Chardonnay is a poor match for Lobster Newberg.

However, Champagne supplies the suave creamy mouth feel that would pair to the rich, round creaminess of the dish, yet the wine's tartness cuts richness and decrease heaviness in the food, while at the same time it props-up the flavors in the dish (positive squeeze of lemon test). What's more, Lobster, the king of the shellfish, demands a wine of equal status, and a good quality Champagne exactly fills the bill perfectly.

Champagne with Crusty, Crispy or Puffed-up Foods

Champagne shines with foods that have a crusty, crispy, or puffed-up feeling. The light, frothy feel of the wine reflects to similar traits in the food. Several types of food give this sensation: batter fried items, breaded foods, Melba toast, crackers, fluffy dumplings, meringues, toasted bread, and dishes that incorporate puffed pastry or Phyllo dough. You will discover many other types of dishes that have a "puffed-up or crispy feeling."

Champagne with Light Foods

Because of the extreme lightness of Champagne, it is a great match for very light dishes. Serve Champagne for starters: hors d'oeuvres, light appetizers, dips, crudités, cold cuts, and similar type dishes. Raw, cold items have a greater sense of lightness than cooked or hot items. Such light items match up wonderfully with Champagne—one of the lightest of wines.

Champagne for Breakfast

Breakfast items are very difficult to pair to wines. **Champagne is one of the very few wines that will marry successfully with breakfast dishes**. It especially goes well with the light, crispy feel of such items as fried bacon and toast, or the creamy richness from such dishes as eggs Benedict. Bread dough flavors found most notably in Blanc de Blanc also tie in beautifully to the flavor of fresh bread. In addition, the puffed-up nature of the bread echoes similar features in the light airy mousse of the wine. Champagne is the absolute best wine to serve with egg dishes.

Champagne as a Palate Cleanser

Champagne's bubbles also act as palate cleansers. Substances that cling to the tongue and surfaces of the mouth such as egg yolk, rich creamy cheeses, or thick custard or cream sauces are loosened by the scrubbing action of Champagne's bubbles. This action reduces cloying richness, refreshes the mouth, and improves the sensation is taste.

Champagne as a Dessert Wine

Sweet versions of sparkling wines match beautifully with light desserts. Because of their lightness and tart acidity, light bodied, fruity desserts pair-up exceedingly well with Champagne. Dishes that incorporate red fruity flavors go best with *blanc de noirs*. Dishes with white flesh fruity flavors with *blanc de blancs*. Nevertheless, either type Champagne, or a blend of the two will work with a variety of sweet fruity desserts. Because Champagne is light bodied, the lighter the dessert, the better the match will be.

Champagne's Limitations

Although Champagne is a very versatile beverage, it has its limitations. For some of the heavyweights of foods—especially red meats—it often seems to pall. With dishes such as pot roast, roast of venison, and lamb chops, it doesn't quite seem to be enough; it will work, but a better fit can be found. Most heavy, spicy hot ethnic dishes are out of character for Champagne; however, some ethnic dishes pair-up very favorably. Try a dry sparkling wine with sushi!

Sparkling Wines from Around-the-World

Sparkling wines have a variety of names depending on the country of origin. In Spain the sparkling wine is Cava, in Germany it is Sekt, in Italy it is Spumante or Prosecco. Champagne is the sparkling wine from the Champagne district of France; however, the name can also be applied to sparklers from the United States provided that the place of origin is stated: American Champagne or New York State Champagne. Most consider French Champagne to be the premier sparkling wine. However, sparkling wines from other countries can be of very high quality—many are reasonably priced.

Quiz

Test your knowledge about sparkling wines with this quiz. You'll be surprised how well sparkling wines will go with a vast array of dishes.

Of the following dishes, which pair-up successfully with a quality sparkling wine?

1. Shrimp Tempura (batter fried shrimp and mixed vegetables)
2. Sushi (raw fish, Japanese style)
3. Batter fried sweetbreads
4. Eggs Benedict (English muffin, topped with ham, poached egg, and hollandaise sauce)
5. Cream of shrimp soup
6. Pike quenelles (a puffy fish dumpling) topped with creamy white sauce
7. Seafood Newburg (shellfish in a rich and creamy sherry flavored sauce served over patty shells)
8. Triple cream cheeses on crackers
9. Oysters Rockefeller (oysters on the half shell topped with chopped watercress or spinach, butter, bread crumbs, and then baked)
10. Coquilles St. Jacques (scallops, creamy wine sauce, bread crumbs, served in scallop shell then browned under a broiler)
11. Fritto Misto (Italian dish—a mixed fry composed of batter coated meats and vegetables)
12. Vichyssoise (a rich, creamy potato and leek soup served cold)
13. Angel food cake topped with strawberry sauce. (served with a sweet sparkling wine)
14. New England clam chowder (cream based chowder)
15. Strawberries topped with crème chantilly (whipped cream based dessert)
16. Seafood risotto (a creamy rice dish incorporating a variety of seafood)

Answers

If you said yes to all of the above you were correct. Below are the reasons why.

1. Shrimp Tempura (batter fried shrimp and mixed vegetables): This is a light, batter-fried dish with a positive "squeeze of lemon" test. In addition, batter fried foods have a crispy, puffed up feel that pair to similar qualities in the wine.

2. Sushi (raw fish Japanese style): Cold, raw, and light dishes are perfect with Champagne, one of the lightest of wines. The dish has a positive "squeeze of lemon test," and Champagne is a very tart wine. The particulate nature of the rice in sushi also blends perfectly with the bubbly nature of the wine.

3. Batter fried sweetbreads: The puffed-up nature of batter fried dishes pair-up to similar characteristics in the wine. The dish also has a positive "squeeze of lemon" test.

4. Eggs Benedict (English muffin, ham, poached egg, hollandaise sauce): The creamy nature of the dish reflects to similar sensations in the wine, and the scrubbing action of Champagne's bubbles cleanses palate. Champagne's high acidity will also stand up to the saltiness of the ham.

5. Cream of shrimp soup: Hot soups in general do not pair up particularly well with wine. Both are liquid, and there is a clash between hot *liquid* soup and cold *liquid* wine. Dry Sherry is commonly served with a wide variety of soups because the high alcohol level produces alcoholic heat: it gives a sensation of heat to the mouth. That being said, lets talk about this wine food pairing. The creamy nature of the dish reflects to the creamy mousse of the Champagne, and Champagne's acidity perks up flavor. The shellfish is begging for tart and the soup base is asking for creamy. Champagne is a natural match.

6. Pike quenelles topped with creamy white sauce: The light, puffed-up nature of the fish dumplings and the creamy consistency of the dish reflect to similar characteristics in the wine; additionally, acidity perks up flavors (positive squeeze of lemon test).

7. Seafood Newburg (shellfish in a rich and creamy Sherry flavored sauce served over patty shells): The creamy nature of the dish, and the crunchy and puffed-up nature of the patty shells reflect to the creamy mousse of the Champagne. Additionally, the dish has a positive "squeeze of lemon test" and is benefited by Champagne's acidity and palate scrubbing action.

8. Triple cream cheeses on crackers: Triple cream cheeses have a thick creamy consistency that is benefited by Champagne's palate scrubbing action. Additionally, the creamy mousse reflects to the creamy nature of the cheese. The crunch of the crackers also calls for Champagne.

9. Oysters Rockefeller (oysters on the half shell topped with chopped watercress or spinach, butter, bread crumbs, and then baked): This is a light breaded dish that would be benefited by the crisp acidity in sparkling wines. The crispness and the airy nature of the breading reflect to similar qualities in the wine. The dish also has a positive squeeze of lemon test.

10. Coquilles St Jacques (scallops, creamy wine sauce, bread crumbs, placed in scallop shell then browned under a broiler): The creamy nature of the dish reflects to the creamy mousse of the Champagne. Additionally, the dish is benefited by acidity and Champagne's palate scrubbing action. The crunch from the crusty breadcrumb topping also calls for Champagne.

11. **Fritto Misto (Italian dish—a deep fried dish composed of batter coated meats and vegetables)**: The light, puffed-up, crispy feeling derived from this batter-coated food reflects to similar features in the wine. Champagne's acidity also props-up flavor. If you wished to stay ethnic dry, Prosecco, an Italian sparkler would make a great match.

12. Vichyssoise (a rich, creamy potato and leek soup served cold): The cold, creamy nature of the soup reflects to similar features in the wine.

13. Angel food cake topped with strawberry sauce: This light, airy cake topped with a light fruity sauce pairs marvelously with the creamy mousse, fruit, and light nature of Champagne. An Italian sparkler called Brachetto d'Acqui has a wonderful sweet, strawberry flavor and a quality mousse. These traits reflect beautifully to the dish. Don't use a dry sparkler with sweet desserts; the sweetness in the dessert will accentuate the tartness in the wine, and the wine will be perceived to be out of balance.

14. New England clam chowder (cream based chowder): The creamy nature of the dish reflects to the creamy mousse of the Champagne, and Champagne's acidity perks up flavor. The clams are calling for tart, and the soup base is asking for creamy. Champagne is a natural choice.

15. Strawberries topped with crème Chantilly: Sweetened whipped cream and strawberries are a natural match-up with a sweet styled Blanc de noirs Champagne. The strawberry flavors so often found in Blanc de noirs echo the same flavor in the dish, and the round, creamy mousse reflects to the whipped cream in the dessert. The Italian sparkler, Brachetto d'Acqui would also be a fabulous match.

16. Seafood risotto: The creaminess of the sparkling wine reflects to the creaminess of the rice. The dish has a positive "squeeze of lemon test" and benefits from the high level of acidity in the wine.

CHAPTER 16
Desserts

Madeline, a sweet little tart

When you match a wine with desserts, the same principles apply as with any other wine-food pairing: you match the qualities of the wine to that of the food. However, sweetness and richness now plays dominant roles. As you would expect, big, rich, heavy desserts go best with wines with similar qualities, but be forewarned: too big of a wine matched with too big of a dessert may produce a sensation of cloying richness. In such instances, make sure that the accompanying wine has sufficient acidity to lighten the match.

Very sweet desserts are often difficult to pair with food, as it can be difficult to find a wine sweet enough to stand-up to the coupling without becoming cloyingly rich. **Remember to keep the sweetness of the wine equal to or greater than that of the food.** If the food is sweeter than the wine, the acidity of the wine will appear to be accentuated, which will make the wine appear thin, weak, and tart. Although this effect is purely psychological, the impact on the pairing is very real. Some people have advocated pairing dry wines, such as Cabernet Sauvignon and Zinfandel to dessert items. Indeed, it has become a trend. This is risky business; however, if the dessert is minimally sweet, the sweetness derived from the alcohol in the wine may be sufficient to support such a match. In most instances, a better choice can be found.

German Riesling

Riesling makes one of the lightest and tartest dessert wines, and they have a great range of sweetness. Kabinett is the least sweet, then, in increasing order of sweetness—Spätlese, Auslese, Eiswein, Beerenauslese (BA), and Trockenbeerenauslese (TBA). TBA's are very sweet, unctuous, and style-wise similar to cordials. However, they are not as heavy, and are much more refined, sophisticated, and complex. They are a marvelous dessert all by themselves. Beerenauslese wines are a little less sweet but are still gifted with a bevy of rich, complex flavors. Eiswein has more tartness and less richness than either Beerenauslese or Trockenbeerenauslese, which makes Eiswein an ideal partner for light desserts that have a high degree of associated tartness. However TBA, BA, and Eiswein are very expensive. If the dessert is not too sweet, a Spätlese or Auslese will often make a great match, and these wines are very reasonable priced.

Rieslings have solid levels of crisp acidity, low alcohol, and bright, well-focused fruity flavors. Because of their light body, low alcohol (many are in the range of 7%), firm acidity, and wide range of sweetness, they are very versatile wines for a wide variety of desserts. However, **Riesling's best match is with light, tart, fruity desserts**. Serve them with apple strudel, peach cobbler, baked apples, lemon tarts, poached pears, and other similarly styled desserts.

Chenin Blanc

The most famous dessert wines made from this varietal come from the Loire Valley in France: **sweet Vouvray, Coteaux du Layon, Quarts de Chaume, and Bonnezeaux**. They are richer and fuller bodied than Rieslings, but still have a solid dose of crisp acidity. The style is somewhat similar to Sauternes, but they are lighter, tarter, and less complex. **Chenin Blanc dessert styled wines make good partners for rich, fruity desserts that have a good component of acidity.** Try them with desserts such as apple pie, pineapple upside-down cake, tortes, and trifles.

Sauternes, the king of dessert wines

Sauternes

Sauternes are the most famous and most refined of all the dessert styled wines. They are richer and less acidic than either Riesling or Chenin Blanc dessert wines, but more intricate.

Sauternes are big, opulent wines that have a regal finesse unmatched by any other wine in its class. They are without question the "kings of dessert wines" These complex wines are loaded with a sophisticated array of exotic scents and flavors. **Serve Sauternes with rich, elaborate desserts where fruit is not a dominant ingredient.** They are great partners for such desserts as *Crème Brûlée, Crème Caramel,* pumpkin flan, cheesecake, and blue cheeses. Sauternes are a perfect match with *Crème Brûlée.* In fact, one of the flavors found in Sauterne's profile is *Crème Brûlée.* These wines are so rich and sophisticated that they make an outstanding dessert all by themselves.

Muscat

There are several different varieties of Muscat grapes. One of the more famous is **Muscat de Beaumes-de-Venise**, a variety grown in the Rhône Valley. It is a rich and very sweet wine fortified with brandy to an alcohol level of at least 15 %.

Many of the Muscat wines have a distinct orange scent and flavor. In California this varietal is called **Orange Muscat.** Because orange and chocolate flavors complement each other, **Orange Muscat is a great choice to pair with chocolate desserts**.

Muscats are sweeter than Sauternes, yet they have a good complement of acidity, which prevents them from becoming cloying. Because of their high degree of sweetness, **Muscats make excellent**

wines to match to very sweet desserts. Although they can be very fine wines, they do not have the finesse or stature of top quality Sauternes. Serve Muscats with desserts such as bread pudding; chocolate cream pie; chocolate candies, , pumpkin pie, chocolate cake, Bananas Foster, Tiramisu or a variety of orange, ginger, or coffee flavored desserts.

Sweet Sherry, Malaga, and Pedro Ximénez

Because of their rich full-body, the sweet versions of these Spanish wines have limited use in wine-food pairings. Sweet Sherries work best with rich desserts that have flavors of dried fruits, nuts, butterscotch, caramel, and chocolate. Serve them with liquor infused fruitcakes, minced meat pie, and rich desserts topped with maple syrup, butterscotch topping, caramel sauce or similar styled desserts.

Malaga and Pedro Ximénez (PX) are very sweet and have a tendency to be cloying, especially when paired with rich and heavy desserts. Cream sherry, made by blending PX Sherry with Oloroso, can also be cloying and have limited use in pairing with desserts.

Port

Like Sherry, Port is full-bodied and very rich. These characteristics limit its use to similarly styled desserts. They have an affinity for rich desserts with flavors of berries, blackcurrants, cherries, figs, dried fruits, raisins, chocolate and nuts. Ports are good partners for desserts such as chocolate cake, fruitcake, chocolate chip cookies, nuts, nut rolls, blue cheeses. Vintage Port is a complete dessert in and of itself.

Madeira

Bual and Malmsey are the most popular styles of Madeira for pairing with desserts. These are very rich and full-bodied wines that have a distinctive scorched flavor, The tartness associated with Madeira is often incongruous with the round, smooth nature of many rich desserts. Rich tart desserts or desserts that are flavored with coffee, toffee, chocolate, caramelized sugar, or nuts blend wonderfully with the flavors in Madeira. Try Madeira with baked caramelized apples, fruitcakes, sugar-glazed nuts, blue cheeses, and other similarly styled desserts.

Champagne and other Sparklers

Sweet styled Champagnes (Sec, Demi-sec, Doux) are versatile, but work best with sweet desserts that have a light, airy nature. Desserts incorporating puffed pastry, or filo dough such as apple crisps, or baklava make good matches, as do creamy desserts such as Zabaglione, or creampuffs. At the present time, sweet Champagnes are somewhat unfashionable, and sometimes difficult to obtain. Sweet sparklers from other countries are more available. However, beware of Italy's popular sparkling wine, Asti Spumante, as it has a tendency to be cloying.

Vin Santo

Vin Santo is an Italian wine made from Malvasia and Trebbiano grapes. Its spicy-apricot-orange flavor is seasoned by a slight oxidized note (somewhat similar to Sherry) that in no way detracts from the wine. This is a rich, complex and full-bodied wine. Alcohol levels sometimes reaches 16%. They are particularly good with dishes incorporating nuts. Many of the wines are ordinary; others can be spectacular. Try Vin Santo with fruitcakes, cookies, streusel topped apricot tort, biscotti, rich chocolate cake and other like styled desserts.

Other Dessert Wines

Zinfandel made in a style similar to Port, is very rich, high in alcohol, and has concentrated spicy-berry flavors. Use it in a manner similar to Port.

An interesting wine made in Australia called **liqueur Muscat** is a rich and exceedingly sweet wine—the sweetest of the Muscats. A little of this wine goes a long way. It blends particularly well with rich, very sweet desserts.

Quiz

Match the wine with the dessert that would make the most successful match. In many cases, one or more other selections would also work quite well. However, select the one that you feel to be the best match.

1. Chocolate cake: (a) LBV Port, (b) Riesling Kabinett, (c) Madeira, (d) Vouvray

2. Baked tart apples (apples, brown sugar): (a) Brut Champagne, (b) Vintage Port, (c) Madeira, (d) M-S-R Auslese

3.   Rhubarb pie (sweet, tart, and tangy): (a) Cream Sherry, (b) Sauternes, (c) sweet styled Zinfandel, (d) M-S-R Riesling Auslese

4.   Crème Brûlée: (a) Sauternes, (b) Riesling Kabinett, (c) Madeira, (d) Muscat de Beaumes-de-Venise

5.   Stilton cheese: (a) Sauternes, (b) Bonnezeaux, (c) Riesling Auslese, (d) Fino Sherry

6.   Chocolate-orange Torte: (a) Orange Muscat, (b) Vin Santo, (c) Sauternes, (d) TBA

7.   Apple strudel: (a) Sauternes, (b) Eiswein, (c) Madeira, (d) Muscat de Beaumes-de-Venise

8.   Sicilian cheese cake (ricotta cheese, triple sec liqueur, candied orange peel, bitter chocolate): (a) Orange Muscat, (b) Muscat de Beaumes-de-Venise, (c) Vin Santo, (d) Liqueur Muscat

9.   Bitter chocolate nut torte with Blackberry Glazing (a dessert with restrained sweetness): (a) Sauternes, (b) Eiswein, (c) TBA, (d) Zinfandel

10.   French Pillows (baked meringue topped with strawberry syrup and whipped cream: (a) Cream Sherry, (b) Rosé Champagne, Demi-sec, (c) Madeira, (e) Sauternes

11.   Cheesecake with caramel topping (a) Sauternes, (b) TBA, (c) Riesling Kabinett, (d) Vintage Port

12.   Pecan pie (a) Malmsey Madeira, (b) cream Sherry, (c) Riesling Kabinett, (d) Eiswein

13.   Boccone Dolce: (This is a luscious Italian refrigerator cake from Sardi's composed of three sweetened meringue layers separated by whipped cream and sliced strawberries and drizzled with melted bittersweet chocolate.): (a) Sauternes, (b) Eiswein, (c) TBA, (d) Brachetto d'Acqui—this is a strawberry flavored Italian sparkler that has a very fine creamy moose.

Answers

The answers below represent the best match to the dessert; in many cases, one or more other selections would also work very well.

1. Chocolate cake: (a) LBV Port: This is a rich dessert whose flavors are compatible with chocolate. The Madeira and Vouvray are a little too tart. The Riesling is too light and too tart. Vouvray and Riesling are not particularly good with chocolate.

2. Baked apples: (apples, brown sugar) (c) Madeira: the baked flavor and the scorched sugar and caramel that form at the bottom of the apple are a great match for Madeira. Brut Champagne is dry and would be a poor match. However, M-S-R Auslese would also be a good choice.

3. Rhubarb pie (sweet, tart, and tangy): (d) M-S-R Riesling Auslese: This is a tart dessert of moderate weight that needs a wine with plenty of acidity. M-S-R Riesling Auslese is the tartest of the bunch.

4. Crème Brûlée: (a) Sauternes: This is an elegant, rich dessert that deserves a wine of stature. Sauternes are rich, sophisticated and the actual flavor of the dessert is present in the flavor profile of the wine. Madeira has a scorched sugar flavor that reflects to the baked sugar crust on top of the custard, but the wine is a little tart for the dish, and it does not reflect the roundness of the custard as well as Sauternes. Muscat de Beaumes-de-Venise makes a good match, but the flavors don't match as well and it lacks the stature of Sauternes.

5. Stilton cheese: (a) Sauternes: Both the wine and cheese have great richness, and the sweetness of Sauternes is a great foil to the saltiness of this great dessert cheese. Bonnezeaux is not quite as rich, but would also make a great match. Riesling Auslese will work, but it lacks the richness of the Sauternes. Fino Sherry is not a dessert wine.

6. Chocolate-orange torte: (a) Orange Muscat: The pronounced orange flavors in Orange Muscat make it the best choice. Orange flavor is very compatible with chocolate. Vin Santo would also work very well.

7. Apple strudel: (b) Eiswein: This is a German styled dessert—stay ethnic. It is a relatively light, tart, and fruity dessert, which make it a great partner for the light, tart, and fruity nature of the wine.

8. Sicilian cheese cake (ricotta cheese, triple sec liqueur, candied orange peel, bitter chocolate): Orange Muscat, Muscat de Beaumes-de-Venise, and liqueur Muscat would all work very well, but the best choice is (c) Vin Santo—Italian—stay ethnic whenever possible.

9. Bitter chocolate nut torte with blackberry glazing (a dessert with restrained sweetness): (d) Zinfandel: Because of the restrained sweetness in the dessert, a dry Zinfandel would likely work. With increased sweetness, move to a Port styled Zinfandel. The berry flavors in the wine are compatible with chocolate and they reflect to similar flavors in the dessert.

10. French pillows (baked meringue topped with strawberry syrup and whipped cream): (b) Rosé Champagne, Demi-sec: This is a light dessert that calls for a light-bodied wine. The airiness of the whipped cream and meringue reflect to the mousse in the Champagne, and the strawberry flavors in the wine echo similar flavors in the dessert. In addition, the ethnicity of the dessert matches that of the wine.

11. Cheesecake with caramel topping (a) Sauternes: Just like the dessert, Sauternes are rich and full-bodied. The flavor of caramel is common in the wine and reflects to the caramel topping in the dessert. Because the cake is served cold, its richness is decreased and the combination is not likely to be cloying.

12. Pecan pie (a) Malmsey Madeira is a good match. The scorched and caramelized flavors tie into the flavors of the dessert, and the wine's firm levels of acidity prevent the combination from becoming cloying. Pecan pie is very rich and sweet, and Cream Sherry could well generate a feeling of excess. The other wines are fruity, and do not fit as well with the flavors in the dessert.

13. Boccone dolce: (d) Brachetto d'Acqui: This is the perfect match. The meringue and the whipped cream are puffed up, which makes this the perfect combination for sparkling wines. The flavors of strawberry in the wine reflect to those in the dessert.

CHAPTER 17
Difficult Foods

*"Don't be difficult Mr. Goldstein – Try one;
I'm sure you'll like it.*

Certain foods are difficult to match with wine. This chapter will help you negotiate through the pitfalls in matching wine with these challenging foods.

Salads

Cold green leaf salads with vinaigrette dressing need light wines with high levels of good crisp acidity. Cold temperature and acidification from salad dressings give salads a very light feeling, even if they are embellished with food items such as fish, shellfish, beef, or even duck. Therefore, a light, tart styled white wine is called for. Remember to keep the acidity of the wine greater than that of the salad to prevent the wine from tasting flat taste.

Vinegar is a product of a spoiled wine. Therefore, its use in a salad dressing will tend to give any accompanying wine the taste of spoilage. Instead of using vinegar as the tart ingredient in a salad dressing, use a tart wine instead. This will not only remove the vinegary taste in the dressing, but it will give an accompanying wine a focus to tie to.

Do not use high priced wines when matching foods to vinegary salad dressings. Unblended and unoaked Sauvignon Blanc wines (Sancerre, Pouilly Fumé, or New Zealand Sauvignon Blanc), Verdicchio, Vouvray, Soave, or other light, tart wines make good choice. For fancy salads such as Caesars Salad you might choose a light tart wine with a more noble stature such as Chablis—but don't get too fancy, and keep the price down.

If the dressing or the salad itself has sweetness, pick a light wine with residual sugars such as Riesling Kabinett or Spätlese. Sweetness in the wine assuages acidity and reflects to the sweet nature of the dish. Matching the sweet taste in wine to that in the accompanying food will strengthen the tie between wine and food.

Soups

Soups are another difficult item to match to wines. The *hot-liquid* nature of soups conflicts with the *cold-liquid* state of wine. Unless the soup is a main course, you may forgo serving a wine. If you do wish to serve a wine, the paragraphs below will help in your selection.

Fino Sherry has high levels of alcohol, which produces a warm mouth feel. The heat from the wine's alcohol ties into the heat of the soup, which helps to blend the two together. The spicy-nutty flavors of Sherry will also blend with the flavors in a variety of soups, such as consommé, turtle soup, liver dumpling soup, French onion soup, and minestrone. Fino, Manzanilla, and Amontillado are good choices; Sercial Madeira, a dry fortified wine Portuguese wine, also has flavors that complement a variety of soups, especially those soups with a little tartness.

Cold soups are less of a problem. Match the flavors, character, and ethnicity of the soup to that of the wine. Wines that have a round, rich mouth feel such as California Chardonnay, Viognier, and Gewürztraminer will work depending on the nature of the main ingredients. However, if the soup is very rich, such full-bodied wines could produce a cloying feeling of excess.

In most cases, it is best to stick to a crisp dry white: Chablis with vichyssoise, chilled fruit soup with M-S-R Riesling Kabinett, chilled vegetable soup with New Zealand Sauvignon Blanc.

Champagne, or any good sparkling wine, is a good alternative for a variety of cream based soups. The creamy mouth feel from its mousse ties into to the creamy nature of the soup, while at the same time, Champagne's tart acidity props-up the flavors of the ingredients in the soup. Try it with New England-styled clam chowder, oyster stew, or lobster bisque.

Hors d'Oeuvres

Most cold hors d'oeuvres will have a sensation of lightness, and will pair best to light to medium bodied wines. Avoid big, heavy, tannic reds. Even heavier items, such as duck and red meats, will have a relative light feel because they are cold and usually served in small amounts with other ingredients such as breads and crackers. Sauvignon Blanc based wines work well, as do Rieslings, Italian whites, Chablis, Pinot Grigio, and Champagne. Light to medium bodied reds, such as Beaujolais, Dolcetto, Pinot Noir, Valpolicella, also make good choices when a red is called for.

Cheeses

Contrary to the popular myth concerning the compatibility cheese and wine, cheeses are not the greatest accompaniments to wine. They interfere with taste by coating the mouth, and their strong flavors conflict with or block out the delicate nuances in wine. **Without doubt, white wines make the best matches to cheeses.**

Cheeses are rich in umami, which accentuates the astringent and flavor suppressing effects of tannins in accompanying wines. Tannic wines block out the flavors in delicate cheeses, and clash with the flavors in strong cheeses. Lighter reds or mature reds with low tannin contents make the best matches. Unfortunately, mature reds are often low in acidity, which makes them poor matches for salty or acidic cheeses.

Many cheeses are high in salt and acidity. In such cases, make sure that these cheeses are served with high acid wines. Low acid wines will become flat and flabby when served with acidic or salty cheeses.

The flavor profile of many cheeses often conflict with wines; they simply don't harmonize with each other. This is true for both the mild and strong flavored cheeses.

Soft cheeses pose an additional problem; they coat the mouth and interfere with the taste sensations. Don't match fine wines with soft cheeses, as there are few synergies with such combinations. Rather the nuances in the wine will often be covered over by the texture and flavors in cheese.

Keep these points in mind as we discuss the interaction of wine with specific types of cheeses.

Hard Cheeses: Most wines pair best with hard cheeses. This is especially true for red wines relatively high in tannins. Mildly flavored hard cheeses will pair successfully with both red and white wines. Soft, round wines with restrained acidity, such as Chardonnay, create a bond with the cheese by echoing its rich creamy texture. The soft round character of mature red wines have a similar effect.

Strong cheeses, the likes of aged cheddar, present a problem with most wines, as their dominant flavors smother and compete with the flavors of wine. Hard cheeses are less likely to develop a cloying rich sensation when paired with fat wines than are soft cheeses.

Soft Cheeses coat the mouth and therefore interfere with the perception of taste. However, if wines are to be served, serve them with wines high in acidity such as Chianti, Beaujolais, Chablis, white Burgundy, Sauvignon Blanc, or Champagne. Fat wines paired to soft cheeses often develop the cloying sensation of excess.

Goat Cheese: There is a strong attraction of this cheese to Sauvignon Blanc. Indeed, dishes that contain even small amounts of goat cheese will often make spectacular marriages to Sauvignon Blanc. Because this cheese is tart and salty, it takes a wine with good levels of acidity to stand up to the aggressive character of the cheese. Pouilly Fumé, Sancerre, and New Zealand Sauvignon Blanc make the best matches because of their high levels of acidity and lack of oak aging. Goat's Cheese is not enhanced by fruity flavors, so wines like Riesling and Beaujolais are not good choices.

Blue Cheese: Sweet wines are the best partners for blue cheeses. Rich, sweet, full-bodied wines such as Sauternes, Port, Bual and Malmsey Madeira, and Tokay Aszu make great matches. Be careful of strong blue cheeses such as Gorgonzola; they are simply too strong to pair with wine. Dessert styled Rieslings will work with mild flavored blue cheeses, but not as well as richer and fuller bodied wines. Stilton with vintage Port and Roquefort with Sauternes are classic matches. The powerful flavors in Blue Cheeses do not work well with dry table wines.

Smoked Cheeses: Most wines are encumbered by the smoky flavor in cheese. It's best not to serve smoky cheeses with wines. Sauvignon Blanc or Gewurztraminer probably works the best.

WINE SELECTION FOR CHEESES		
CHEESE STYLE	**PROBLEM**	**BEST WINE CHOICE**
Hard Cheese—mild	Flavors in the cheese compete with the flavors in the wine.	Low tannic red White wines preferred
Hard Cheese—strong	Flavors in the cheese compete with the flavors in the wine. Cheeses are high in umami which augments the flavor suppression effect of tannins and causes tannins to become bitter or metallic tasting.	Flavorful, low tannic red—White wines preferred
Soft Cheeses	Coat the mouth and interfere with the perception of taste	Best with high acid wines, especially Champagne—white wines preferred.

Goat Cheese	Cheese is salty and acidic	Strong affinity Sauvignon Blanc. Lighter styled high acid whites, and light, low tannic reds will also work but not as well.
Blue Cheese	Cheese is rich, very flavorful, and full-bodied. No wine can stand up to the salty and aggressive flavors in Gorgonzola or similarly crafted cheeses	Full bodied sweet wines: Port, Sauternes, Bual and Malmsey Madeira, and Tokay Aszu
Smoked Cheeses	Wines flavors are encumbered by smoky flavor	Sauvignon Blanc or Gewurztraminer

Figure 24

Other Difficult Foods

Sweet sauces and condiments present a problem when serves with dry red table wines. As you will recall, one should always keep the sweetness of the wine equal to or greater than the sweetness of the food. The only sweetness in dry wines comes from alcohol and the perception of ripe fruity flavors. Ripe, fruity young wines, such as Beaujolais or fruit dominated Australian Shiraz, will increase the impression of sweetness, and in most cases will pair to subtly sweet foods. Riesling Kabinett or Spätlese and sweet styled Sauvignon Blanc wines are good choices if the sweetness is overt, and if they fit the character of the dish.

Sweetness tends to cling to the palate longer than most of the other taste sensations, and it can carry over to subsequent wines.

A bite of bread will help to readjust the palate after tasting a sweet wine or food.

Mint and **chocolate** are formidable palate deadeners, especially in a sweet sauce. It is best not to serve mint sauce with items such as lamb if they are accompanied by wine. Besides, what do you want to taste—mint or lamb?

Chocolate is more forgiving, but you must be careful of what types of wine you choose. As most chocolate items are quite sweet, a dessert styled wine is called for. The flavor of chocolate pairs well with berry fruits, such as blackberries, raspberries, currants, and cherries. It also blends well with the flavors of orange. Wines such as Orange Muscat, desert styled Pinot Gris, Port styled Zinfandel and Port are good choices.

Dry wines, such as Zinfandel and Cabernet Sauvignon are often recommended to match with sweet chocolate desserts, and if the dessert has minimal sweetness, they will work. But with overtly sweet desserts, they are a failure as the palate deadening effect of the combination of chocolate and sweetness hammers the wine.

Vinegar used to acidify foods follows the same scenario as in the discussion under salads. It fights with wines, because vinegar is a product of wine spoilage. Use tart wines such as Sancerre, Vouvray, and Pouilly Fumé, and do not serve expensive wines with any dish in which the flavor of vinegar is obvious. As an alternative, many chefs will use tart wine or citrus juice in place of vinegar in dishes that need to be acidified. Instead of using vinegar as the acidifying agent, use a little Sancerre to provide tartness.

Artichokes make wine taste sweet. This is due to the reaction of wine with a chemical in artichokes called cynarin. Joanna Simmons recommends squeezing a few drops of fresh lemon juice on the artichoke, which usually alleviates the problem.

The bold green flavors in vegetables, such as **asparagus, bell peppers, spinach** and the like, are not complimentary to most wines; however, they do have a special affinity for light, dry Sauvignon Blanc based wines.

Soy sauce, fish sauce, or other salty sauces and condiments can be a problem because of their high salt content. Dishes containing such salty items will require wines with high acidity. These substances are also high in umami, which accentuates the tannins in red wines, so it is best to stick with light, tart white wines. New Zealand or Chilean Sauvignon Blanc, Chablis, or lighter styled Chardonnay make good matches. If you prefer a red, try wines like Chinon, Valpolicella, Bardolino, or lighter styled Cabernet Franc.

Palate coating foods such as egg yolk, mayonnaise, soft creamy cheeses, hollandaise sauce, and similarly textured foods need wine with crisp acidity. Acidity lighten the weight of the food and cleans the palate. White wines work best—sparkling wines in particular. Champagne's cleansing bubbles are a great foil for palate clinging sauces, yet their creamy mousse ties into the creamy nature of the sauce. Asparagus with a rich hollandaise sauce finds a perfect match with the green flavors in a Sauvignon Blanc; Eggs Benedict works will with Brut Champagne, and shrimp with a rich, creamy tartar sauce is invigorated with the lemony freshness of Chablis.

Smoked fish or highly flavored oily fish will clash with most wines. Choose a simple, light, dry, tart, inexpensive white wines such as Verdicchio, Trebbiano, Soave, Muscadet, Pinot Grigio, Sauvignon Blanc, or Pouilly Fumé. Sparkling wines will work particularly well with dishes that have a creamy component such as bagels and lox (smoked salmon) with cream cheese. Smoky flavors have an affinity to sweet wines. Riesling Kabinett or Spätlese can pair surprisingly well with a variety of smoked fish,

Ice Cream: The trick here is to use the wine to mimic an ice cream topping. A very sweet wine is required such as Australian liqueur Muscat, Muscat de Beaumes-de-Venise, a ripe California Orange Muscat, or Pedro Ximénez. Match the flavors in the ice cream with the flavors in the wine. Try Pedro Ximénez with caramel swirled or nutty flavored ice cream, Orange Muscat with chocolate ice cream, and Australian liqueur Muscat with fruity flavored ice creams. Because of the ice-cold nature of ice cream, the development of a cloying sensation of excess in unlikely.

Quiz

Which of the following will make good wine-food pairings?

1. Young Barolo and Gorgonzola cheese
2. Fino Sherry and turtle soup
3. Mixed green salad, hearts of palm, candied walnuts, mandarin orange segments, topped with a sweet tart orange flavored dressing served with Riesling Kabinett
4. Mild cheddar cheese and mature red Bordeaux
5. Grilled shrimp stuffed with feta cheese, herbs, and breadcrumbs served with Sauvignon Blanc
6. Cold grilled noisette (small round slice) of pork topped with a slice of sautéed green apple (served as an hors d'oeuvres) with Riesling Kabinett
7. Cold asparagus spears wrapped with a thin slice of roast beef (served as an hors d'oeuvres) paired with Sauvignon Blanc

8.   Salad Niçoise (tomatoes, olives, garlic, anchovies, green beans, onions, tuna, hard-boiled eggs, and herbs) served with Sauvignon Blanc

9.   Creamed shrimp chowder with Brut Champagne

10.   Pigs in blankets (tiny sausages wrapped in pie dough) and Beaujolais

11.   California roll (sushi) with a dry sparkling California wine.

12.   Chocolate Cake with a Port styled Zinfandel

13.   Bonnezeaux and Stilton Cheese

14.   Asparagus spears wrapped in pastry and Sauvignon Blanc

15.   Seviche (raw fish marinated in citrus juice) and Verdicchio

Answers

All are good choices except for #1. Barolo is a big, rich, tannic wine. Gorgonzola is rich in umami, and umami augments the astringent and flavor suppressing effects of tannin. The wine will appear more tannic and will develop a metallic taste. There are very few wines that will stand up to the powerful flavors in Gorgonzola

CHAPTER 18
At the Restaurant

Gentlemen, you're all so delightful...and I have so many choices!

There are many choices to consider when you match a wine to food; it is up to you to pick the best one. It is rare that you can make connections to all of the facets that couple wine to food, but the more links that you can establish, the more successful the wine-food marriage will be.

Someone might choose different qualities to link a wine to a food than you did. That doesn't mean that he is wrong, and you are right. You may have used texture and flavor characteristics in your wine-food integration for a particular dish, while someone else might have chosen to use ethnicity, weight, and ambiance. You both may have come up with very good matches using very different wines. There are often many choices. As long as you adhere to the general principals outlined in this book, the manner in which you tie a wine to a food is purely a matter of your own creativity. Matching wine with food is an artistic endeavor, and people will often vary in their choices in expressing their version.

Many random wine-food pairings will be acceptable without any before thought. They may not be great marriages, but they are workable. However, we are looking for more than just an acceptable match; we are striving to create synergistic wine-food pairings, where the pleasure derived from the union of wine plus food is greater than the sum of the individual parts.

There are many instances, however, when the marriage between wine and food will overtly clash. In some cases, the wine overpowers the food by obscuring flavors and throwing the combination out of balance, or the wine's balance is encumbered by high salt, tartness, or sweetness in the food. In other instances, the union of wine and food might create a heavy, cloying feeling of excess. Such counterproductive marriages of wine and food are inexcusable. It is shocking that many chefs that have graduated from first-class culinary schools haven't the faintest idea about the technique of matching wine with food. The fact that many culinary schools across the nation have no training or only minimal training in the art of matching wine with food is incredible.

The Restaurants Responsibility

When you are dining at a restaurant, you are restricted to the wines on the restaurant's wine list. In some situations you can be somewhat hampered in selecting a wine for a particular dish, because many restaurants have a limited selection of food friendly wines. Chardonnay is often the dominant white. If you are lucky, you might find a Sauvignon Blanc, and there are frequently no sweet fruity white wines available. For the reds, California Cabernet Sauvignon is usually readily available, but Pinot Noir, Zinfandel, red Burgundy, and red Bordeaux are often missing or sparsely represented. Often you are forced to choose the best wine from a mediocre selection of wines.

A high quality restaurant will have a wide variety of food-friendly wines that fit the context of their menu. The types of wine and their price should be varied in a spectrum that allows for an eclectic selection, yet minor concessions in quality should be made so that the wines fit the price range of the full spectrum of diners.

Good chefs make wine-food marriage as artistic as possible by tweaking their food so that it interacts with wine along as many facets at possible. They might add a flavor in the food that can be reflected to a similar flavor in the wine, or perhaps they may sweeten the food so that it will better marry to a sweet styled wine.

The Chef might apply a fruity glaze to duck, or serve chicken with a fruity relish so that these flavors can reflect to similar flavors in the wine. Beets work will with Pinot Noir, asparagus and green vegetables tie into Sauvignon Blanc, cherries and herbs go well with California Merlot, and peaches and apricots work well with Rieslings. Just a little dab of flavor in a dish is enough to accent it sufficiently to blend with a specific wine style.

If the food is spicy-hot, sweet, and fruity, the restaurant should supply a sweet fruity wine that will blend with the character of the food. If the food is big, rich, and robust, have full-bodied wines available, some mature, and others with good levels of acids and tannins. In other words, have wines available that match your menu.

In constructing a menu, some restaurants will include in the price of the meal a wine selection to accompany each dish on the menu. Unfortunately, in many of the restaurants that I have visited, these selections frequently miss the mark. Others will simply recommend a wine for each course. At a minimum, the restaurant should make sure that the wine list includes wines that fit the context of all of the dishes on their menu. A trained staff should be available that is able to help the diner select a proper wine for his meal. Restaurants that have wine-knowledgeable wait staff will increase wine sales dramatically. This will make both the restaurant owner and the diner happy people.

Confusing Combinations

If you own a restaurant, avoid making dishes with conflicting ingredients that will encumber your wine selection. One such classic is "Steak and Lobster." Besides not being very imaginative, the two ingredients really don't complement each other, and they call for two different styled wines. A rich full-bodied Cabernet Sauvignon would work great for the steak, but it would pulverize the lobster. The lobster is looking for a light, crisp, tart wine, perhaps with a trace of sweetness, which is not particularly ideal for the steak. Sure, we can pick a wine that will be acceptable for both dishes, but mediocrity is not what we are striving for. Don't frustrate your customers with such confusing combinations. Rather, make dishes in which the wine will add to the enjoyment of the dish, not merely go with it. Make the dining experience as pleasurable as possible. After all, isn't that why the customer came to the restaurant in the first place?

Unfortunately, we are sometimes forced to make compromises. Suppose your wife ordered lobster, and you ordered steak, but you can afford only one bottle of wine. Now you have a problem. However, had you used your head, you should have ordered a dish that would be more wine friendly in regard to her dish. Of course, you can always order wine by the glass; however, you have no assurance as to how long the bottle has been opened. The longer a bottle has been opened and the lower the level of wine in the bottle, the more likely it is that the wine's flavors have dissipated.

Let us assume that you are the waiter or sommelier; the couple made their choice, and it is up to you to recommend a wine. He wants steak and she wants lobster. You suggest that the gentleman make an alternate selection; however, he is in no mood to be chivalrous. He wants his steak!

In such situations, always select a wine that will match to the lightest dish, in this case, the lobster. Keep Champagne in mind, it will go with a great variety of dishes. However, with steak, it is not particularly attractive. A white Burgundy would go very well with lobster, and although it may not be your first choice for the steak, it would certainly go with it. It's refreshing tart acidity would invigorate the flavors in both dishes. With the lobster, it has a positive "squeeze of lemon test" and the wine's buttery flavor would reflect to the dipping-butter that accompanies the lobster. The spark of acidity provided by the wine would bolster the flavors in the steak, but something is missing. The wine is great for the lobster. However, with the steak it misses a beat or two; it doesn't clash, but with the steak, it is certainly not a synergistic match.

In dishes that have major and minor elements, such as filet mignon stuffed with crabmeat, there is simply no match that will hit the jackpot. Restaurants should not force their patrons into compromising situations in regard to wine selection.

The Dining Experience

I hope that you now feel more comfortable with matching a wine with food. All that it takes is a little practice. Here are a few challenges to get you started. If you do not agree with my choices, or the reasoning behind them, that's acceptable. Make your own selection—but be prepared to back it up! This little review will help you tie together everything that you have learned. Let's start with a dinner party at home and work our way up to restaurants. At home you have more leeway as you have control of both wine and food.

Dinner Party at Home

Select a wine to match the following entrees:

Entree

1. Grilled shrimp with a spicy, sweet and tart apricot glaze
2. Tuna steak with baby beets and fried rice cakes
3. Linguini with white clam sauce and topped with steamed baby clams
4. Veal Piccata—veal, lemons, capers served with risotto and vegetables

5. Corned beef, cabbage, potatoes, and root vegetables

6. Broiled duck breast, topped with an unsweetened wild cherry sauce, mashed potatoes, vegetables

7. Beef Burgundy— beef braised in red wine, onions, mushrooms, baby potatoes

8. Poached eggs on toasted English muffins topped with hollandaise sauce, deep-fried potato cakes, chorizo sausage.

9. Filet Mignon topped with Bordelaise sauce (made with red Bordeaux wine) and morel mushrooms, twice baked potatoes, French green beans

10. Herb crusted chicken breasts stuffed with feta cheese, capers, and walnuts; roasted bell peppers stuffed with tomatoes, pine nuts, and rice; oven baked asparagus spears.

Answers:

To understand the reasoning for selecting the wine, focus on the underlined words:

1. **Grilled <u>shrimp</u> with a <u>spicy,</u> <u>sweet</u> and <u>tart</u> <u>apricot</u> glaze—** *light weight dish that is sweet, tart and spicy with flavors of apricot. Match with a fruity, sweet, tart, light weight wine with white-fruit flavors—**<u>German Riesling Kabinett</u>***

2. **<u>Tuna</u> steak with baby <u>beets</u> and fried rice cakes—**This is a *medium weight dish with flavors of beets. A medium weight wine with flavors of beets would work perfectly.—**<u>Pinot Noir, Oregon</u>***

3. **<u>Linguini</u> with white <u>clam</u> sauce topped with steamed baby <u>clams</u>—**think ethnic (Italian varietal), lightweight clams call for a tart, citrus flavored wine (positive squeeze of lemon test)—**<u>Pinot Grigio</u>** or **<u>Soave</u>** (a tart, citrus flavored, light wines). A dry Italian sparkling wine would also work such as **<u>Prosecco</u>**.*

4. **Veal Piccata—<u>veal, lemons, capers</u> served with risotto and vegetables—** *think ethnic (Italian varietal), call for a*

*tart, citrus flavored light-meduim weight wine (reflect the citrus flavor in the wine to that in the dish. Salty capers and tart lemon call for tartness in accompanying wine—**Pinot Grigio**, **Soave** or any other light to medium white Italian varietal*

5. **Corned beef, cabbage, potatoes, and root vegetables**—*This is an unsophisticated dish of medium weight that calls for a similarly styled wine; the dish is rather salty and calls for a wine with good levels of acidity—**Beaujolais***

6. **Broiled duck breast, topped with an unsweetened wild cherry sauce, mashed potatoes, vegetables**—*This is a rich full-bodied dish with flavors of cherries. A full-bodied wine with flavors of cherries would make an ideal match. Reflect the cherry flavors common in California Merlot, a full-bodied wine, to similar flavors in the dish—young **California Merlot.***

7. **Beef Burgundy— beef braised in red wine, onions, mushrooms, baby potatoes**—*This is a French dish from Burgundy. Stay Ethnic. **Red Burgundy, village wine such as Nuits-Saint-Georges, or Gevrey-Chambertin.***

8. **Poached eggs on toasted English muffins topped with hollandaise sauce, deep-fried potato cakes, chorizo sausage.**—*This dish is loaded with creamy, toasty, salty and, fried ingredient,: all characteristics that call for a sparkling wine. Champagne is both creamy and tart, in addition, Champagne is a great palate cleanser (egg yolk)—**Premium California Sparkling wine***

9. **Filet Mignon topped with Bordelaise sauce (made with red Bordeaux wines) and morel mushrooms, twice baked potatoes, French green beans**—*This is a sophisticated, moderate-heavy weight dish that calls for a similar styled wine, Stay ethnic, A sophisticated red Bordeaux wine such as **Château Lunch Bages** will make a smashing match.*

10. **Herb crusted chicken breasts stuffed with feta cheese, capers, and walnuts; roasted bell peppers stuffed with**

tomatoes, pine nuts, and rice; oven baked asparagus spears—*Chicken is medium weight, capers and feta cheese are salty, tomatoes are acidic, all of which call for a tart wine. Herbs and green vegetal flavors reflect to similar flavors in Sauvignon Blanc; dishes with feta cheese work great with Sauvignon Blanc*—**Sauvignon Blanc, New Zealand**

I hope that you felt comfortable in selecting a wine for these dishes. Now that you have your confidence up, lets try our hand at the restaurant.

At the Restaurant

Dining at a restaurant makes wine selection a little more challenging than when putting on a dinner party at home.

You and your significant other are dining at a posh restaurant in New York City. Price is no object—this is a very special occasion. Choose a wine from the wine list to accompany each course. More than one wine selection may work for each entree.

The first exercise assumes that both you and your companion are having the same dish. You only need to concern yourself with one wine-food pairing. The second exercise is a little more difficult. You must select one wine that will accompany both of your dishes.

White Wines

Joseph Drouhin Corton Charlemagne, 2003 (red Burgundy)

Jean-Paul Chablis, 2004 Montmains (white Burgundy)

Bernkastel Doktor, Kabinett 2004 (German Riesling, M-S-R))

Babcock 11 Oaks 2004, Sauvignon Blanc

Pra Soave 2005 (tart Italian white wine)

Veuve Clicquot Brut Champagne

Red Wines

Jamet Côte Rôtie 1998 (premium Syrah based Rhône wine)

Geantet-Pansiot, Gevrey Chambertin 2000 (red Burgundy wine)

Robert Mondavi, Cabernet Sauvignon 2000

Château Léoville Las Cases 1998 (red Bordeaux wine)

Ponzi Pinot Noir Reserve 2004(Oregon Pinot)

Rosenblum Zinfandel (California) 2005

Fleurie Beaujolais 2005

Dessert

Schloss Johannisberg Beerenauslese 2004 (sweet German Riesling)

Chateau Suduiraut Sauternes 2004

Avignonesi Vin Santo 1999 (Italian dessert wine)

Fortified Wines

Alvear Fino Sherry

Dow Vintage Port 1989

Focus on the underlined words. They will guide you in making the proper wine food pairing.

Exercise 1

1. Chicken Kiev (a <u>chicken breast</u> is wrapped around a piece of chilled <u>butter</u> and then dipped in egg and <u>breadcrumbs</u>. The breast is then <u>fried</u>, and when it is cut, the sealed-in melted butter escapes.)

2. Veal <u>Piccata</u> (<u>veal, lemons, capers</u>), risotto, and vegetables

3. New England Clam Chowder (a <u>creamed-based chowder</u>)

4. Roast of <u>venison</u> with <u>rich brown gravy</u> and mashed potatoes

5. <u>Beef Tenderloin</u> topped with a gravy infused with black currants

6. <u>Shrimp</u> with <u>creamy white sauce</u> served in <u>patty shells</u> (puffed pastery)

7. Turtle soup (a <u>hot, rich, thick soup</u> enriched with brown sauce)

8. <u>Barbecued</u> short ribs, fried finger potatoes, fiddle head fern with <u>black pepper flavored</u> butter sauce

9. Mixed <u>green</u> salad, <u>pears</u>, and <u>candied</u> <u>walnuts</u> all topped with a <u>tart</u> and <u>sweet orange</u> flavored dressing.

10. Caesar Salad (Romaine <u>lettuce</u>, garlic <u>vinaigrette</u>, <u>Parmesan cheese</u>, croutons, raw egg, <u>anchovies</u>)

11. Lobster Newberg (<u>Lobster</u> in a <u>rich creamy</u> sauce and served between layers of <u>puffed pastry</u>

12. <u>Linguini</u> with <u>white clam sauce</u> topped with steamed baby clams

13. Crème Carmel (<u>sweet caramel custard</u>)

14. Biscotti (<u>Italian</u> <u>crunchy</u> cookie flavored with <u>almonds</u>, <u>hazelnuts</u>, and anise seed)

15. Broiled <u>duck breast</u> with a <u>sweet</u> and <u>tart</u> <u>apricot</u> glazing, with roasted potatoes, peas

16. Poached <u>eggs</u> on <u>English muffins</u> topped with <u>hollandaise sauce</u>, deep <u>fried</u> potato cakes, <u>chorizo</u> <u>sausage</u>

17. <u>Shrimp</u> with a <u>sweet</u> and <u>spicy-hot</u> <u>pineapple</u> flavored sauce

18. Black Angus roast <u>beef</u>, mashed potatoes and <u>gravy</u>, green beans

19. Grilled <u>Tuna</u> topped with <u>cranberry</u> chutney, fried rice cakes, carrots

20. <u>Filet Mignon</u> topped with <u>a rich brown gravy</u> sauce and morel <u>mushrooms</u>, Duchesse potatoes, <u>French</u> green beans

21. <u>Pork</u> roast stuffed with <u>cherries</u> (<u>unsweetened</u>), rice and nuts; buttered baby new potatoes, sautéed summer squash

22. <u>Herb</u> crusted <u>chicken</u> breasts stuffed with <u>feta cheese</u>, <u>capers</u>, and walnuts; roasted <u>green</u> bell peppers stuffed with <u>tomatoes</u>, pine nuts and rice; oven artichoke hearts

23. <u>Apple</u> <u>strudel</u> topped with <u>whipped cream</u>

24. <u>Fried breaded</u> <u>oysters</u> topped with Nantua sauce (<u>cream sauce</u> flavored with crayfish butter, <u>white</u> <u>wine</u>, tomatoes, cognac) and served on <u>crispy</u> toast point

25. <u>Crab</u> cakes (chopped crab, herbs, eggs)

26. Crown roast of <u>lamb</u> stuffed with breadcrumbs, <u>black currants</u>, onions and <u>herbs</u>, fried potato cakes, and mixed grilled vegetables

27. <u>Dover sole</u> with <u>lemon butter</u> sauce and slivered walnuts, buttered noodles, yellow summer squash

Answers

In many of these dishes, several of the wines will work. The selections below are my own biases.

1. Joseph Drouhin Corton Charlemagne or Veuve Clicquot Brut Champagne

2. Pra Soave

3. Veuve Clicquot Brut Champagne

4. Jamet Côte Rôtie (but any of the other reds would also work, but perhaps not quite as well)

5. Robert Mondavi Cabernet Sauvignon

6. Veuve Clicquot Brut Champagne

7. Alvear Fino Sherry

8. Rosenblum Zinfandel

9. Bernkastel Doktor, Kabinett

10. Jean-Paul Chablis, Montmains (Pra Soave would also work, but not as well)

11. Joseph Drouhin Corton Charlemagne, or Veuve Clicquot Brut Champagne

12. Pra Soave

13. Chateau Suduiraut Sauternes

14. Avignonesi Vin Santo

15. Bernkastel Doktor, Kabinett

16. Veuve Clicquot Brut Champagne

17. Bernkastel Doktor, Kabinett

18. Robert Mondavi, Cabernet Sauvignon (any of the reds would work, Beaujolais would be my last choice)

19. Ponzi Pinot Noir Reserve

20. Château Léoville Las Cases

21. Ponzi Pinot Noir Reserve, or Geantet-Pansiot, Gevrey Chambertin

22. Babcock 11 Oaks, Sauvignon Blanc

23. Schloss Johannisberg Beerenauslese

24. Veuve Clicquot Brut Champagne, or Jean-Paul Chablis, Montmains

25. Babcock 11 Oaks, Sauvignon Blanc or Veuve Clicquot Brut Champagne

26. Château Léoville Las Cases, or Robert Mondavi, Cabernet Sauvignon

27. Jean-Paul Chablis, Montmains, or Babcock 11 Oaks, Sauvignon Blanc

Exercise 2

1. **You:** Escargot á la Bourguignonne (snails) on toast points, with butter, parsley and nutmeg

   Your Date: Mussels in a white wine sauce

2. **You:** Deep-fried scampi, gnocchi (Italian potato dumplings) topped with beurre blanc sauce (butter sauce), and Parmesan cheese, with Italian styled green beans

   Your Date: Lobster Thermidor (Lobster, white sauce, Parmesan cheese)

3. **You:** Lemon-glazed chicken topped with a sweet pineapple and apricot relish, fried potato cakes

   Your Date: Sauerbraten: Braised pickled and spiced pot roast with a gravy flavored with crushed ginger snaps.

4. **You:** Carpaccio (Thin shavings of raw beef topped with olive oil and lemon juice) atop thinly sliced raw onion.

   Your Date: Pike Quenelles (light fish dumplings), topped with a creamy white sauce.

5. **You:** Grilled swordfish with onions, garlic mashed potatoes, green beans.

   Your Date: Filet mignon with wild rice and maple glazed carrots.

6. **You:** Hunch of wild boar, couscous, sweet apple-lemon-peach compote, mixed grilled vegetables.

Your Date: Pork cutlets glazed in a sweet and sour sauce, fried rice patties, apricot-pineapple relish.

7. **You:** Pork roast stuffed with asparagus spears, capers, and breadcrumbs served on top of artichoke hearts and accompanied by sautéed eggplant and red pepper.

   Your Date: Grilled salmon with lemon dill sauce and served with avocado stuffed with crab.

8. **You**: Crème Brûlée (rich pudding topped with caramelized sugar crust)

   Your Date: Rich white cake with butter-cream frosting

Answers

1. Joseph Drouhin Corton Charlemagne, or Jean-Paul Chablis, Montmains,: These are both light-medium weight dishes. The escargot is prepared in the style of Burgundy; white Burgundy is most appropriate—stay ethnic. The weight and the character of the wines fit both dishes.

2. **Joseph Drouhin Corton Charlemagne, or Jean-Paul Chablis, Montmains**: The lobster, the king of shellfish, demands a high quality white wine. There is good acidity in both wines, and both the shrimp and the lobster have a positive squeeze of lemon test. The gnocchi & shrimp dish is a medium weight dish and the lobster is light to medium weight. Both these dishes are compatible with the weight of these wines. Both have a positive *squeeze of lemon test*. With this selection, we forgo the Italian ethnicity associated with the scampi dish.

3. **Bernkastel Doktor, Kabinett**: The lemon-glazed chicken with sweet pineapple-apricot relish is a sweet dish that requires a sweet wine. The sauerbraten is tart and sweet and calls for a wine with similar characteristics. Although a red meat frequently calls for a heavy dry red wine, this dish calls for a tart and sweet white wine.

4. **Veuve Clicquot Brut Champagne**: The light airy fish dumplings are a perfect match with Champagne. Light puffed-up foods work great with Champagne. Carpaccio is cold very thin shavings of beef that, in this case, is flavor with olive oil and lemon juice. Both the cold nature of the dish and the acidification lighten its weight. Both dishes are light to medium weight. The tart citrus flavors in the Champagne reflect to the lemon seasoning of the Carpaccio, and the crisp acidity of the wine brightens the flavors of both dishes.

5. **Ponzi Pinot Noir Reserve**: Here we have a meaty fish and a choice cut of beef. The meaty fish (shark, swordfish, tuna, salmon and like fish) are medium bodied, flavorful fish that do well with medium bodied red wines with restrained tannins. The beef might be happier with a bigger wine, like a Cabernet Sauvignon; however, it is compatible with Pinot Noir based wines as well. The slight sweetness of maple-glazed carrots is a good point of reflection for the soft, sweet nature of Pinot Noir. Gevrey Chambertin, a Pinot Noir based red Burgundy, is an expensive wine and a little heavy for the fish (it is a big masculine styled red Burgundy) but it would work very well with the beef.

6. **Bernkastel Doktor, Kabinett**: Sweet is a dominant taste sensation and therefore this dish calls for a sweet wine. The apple-lemon-peach compote and the apricot-pineapple relish provide sweetness to both of these dishes. The white fruit flavors in both entrees reflect very favorable to the Bernkastel Doktor. The hunch of wild boar is a hardier dish than the glazed pork cutlet, but it will still marry successfully to this wine, Lightweight wines have universal acceptance and will pair successfully to both of these dishes.

7. **Babcock Sauvignon Blanc**: Both dishes are medium weight and abound with green flavors that tie neatly into the green flavors in this medium bodied wine.

8. **Chateau Suduiraut Sauternes**: The flavor of Crème Brûlée is present in the wine and reflects superbly to the Crème

Brûlée dessert. The white cake with the butter cream frosting has a rich creamy consistency and full body that ties into the characteristics of the cake. There is enough acidity in the wine to preclude the combination from becoming cloying.

CHAPTER 19
Odds and Ends

A Wine Tasters Vocabulary

Over the years, a vocabulary has evolved that is used to describe the attributes and faults of a wine. By learning this vocabulary, you will be able to describe what you smell and taste in a clear and distinct fashion; the language is universal. An exchange in dialogue is a great part of the enjoyment in sharing a bottle of wine. The chart below lists some of the common words in a wine tasters vocabulary.

Wine Tasters Terms	
Acidity	The tart aspect of wine due to a group of acids, the predominant ones being tartaric, malic, and lactic acid.
Aftertaste	The taste that lingers in the mouth after the wine has been swallowed.
Aggressive	This is an assertive quality in wine characterized by excessive tartness, or astringency, or both.
Alcoholic	When a wine's alcohol is perceived in the nose or on the palate (heat) the wine is said to be alcoholic.
Angular	Wines that lack roundness. This is due to excessive amounts of acids and/or tannins.
Aroma	The fruity scent of a young wine.

Astringent	Wines with a rough, dry mouth-feel.
Austere	A physiologically young wine in a "bud" like condition. Such wines are tart, tannic, and lacking flavor. There is good likelihood for further development in austere wines.
Backward	A wine that is more youthful appearing than its chronological age.
Balance	A balanced wine is when all elements (acids, tannins, alcohol, etc.) are in the optimal proportions so that at maturity the wine is showing its best.
Blackcurrants	Also known as cassis, this is Cabernet Sauvignon's most frequently identifiable scent.
Beefy	This term denotes a full-bodied wine with high alcohol and extract. They are not necessarily soft and supple.
Body	The magnitude of the substantive feel or weight of a wine as it crosses the palate.
Bouquet	The complex predominantly non-fruity scents that develop as a wine matures in bottle: tobacco, mushrooms truffles, leather, tar, coffee, chocolate, etc.
Breed	A mark of distinction attributable to lineage.
Briery	A wine that is aggressive and spicy (black pepper).
Chewy	High extract wines with thick, viscous texture.
Closed	Wines in a juvenile state. The character of the wine has not fully developed: bud-like.
Complex	Wines with multiple scents and flavors.
Cooked	Grapes that are "baked" by to long exposure to the sun. In such cases the wines are deep in color and have excessive brown tones and stewed, heavy flavors. The term is derogatory.

Corked	Corks infected with cork mold transfer their disparaging scent and flavor to the wine. Such wines have moldy, dank basement, or old wet cardboard smell and flavor. The dank flavor is due to a chemical called TCA.
Diffuse	Wines that have blurry, unfocused flavors. The flavors all run together.
Dumb	Similar to closed and austere, but a little less promising and somewhat derogatory.
Earthy	Wines that have the smell of rich, clean, fresh tilled soil. If the scent is clean and healthy it has a positive connotation; if it is heavy, dirty, and course, it has a negative connotation.
Fat	Full-bodied, concentrated, supple wines that have tempered levels of acids and tannins. These are good drinking wines, but are somewhat difficult to match to food.
Feminine	An anthropomorphic term delineating female traits: delicate, charming, elegant, refined, soft, light, and perfumed.
Finesse	Wines with great breeding and refinement are said to have finesse.
Focused	The scents and flavors in the wine are in focus when they are distinct and clearly discernible.
Forward	Wines whose charms are in a precocious condition—early drinking wines.
Full-bodied	Wines that have a sense of weight that give a full and substantive feel in the mouth. Such wines are high in alcohol and flavorful extract.
Green	Wines made from unripe grapes. Acids are high and flavors are poorly developed. The wines are low in alcohol and lack color. Such wines have vegetal, herbal and grassy scents and flavors. The term is also used for wines that are immature.

Hard	Wines with excessive acids or tannins. Hopefully with time these wines will evolve.
Harsh	A derogatory term: such wines will never evolve.
Heady	Wines high in alcohol—similar to alcoholic.
Hedonistic	Rich, lush wines that evoke a great deal of pleasure.
Hollow	The middle part of the tasting experience is missing. These wines start tasting good then fade out but then return in the finish.
Hot	Wines that taste of excessive alcohol.
Jammy	Wines with very high concentrations of ripe fruity extracts.
Leafy	Wines with very noticeable scents of herbs and leaves.
Lean	The opposite of fat wines: low alcohol and extracts; often high acidity.
Limpid	Crystal clear wines that tend to coruscate light.
Length	Same meaning as aftertaste. It's the persistent flavors that you experience immediately after the wine has been swallowed.
Loose-knit	The flavors and scents are readily discernable.
Masculine	An anthropomorphic term denoting wines with male traits: big, bold, aggressive, assertive, angular, and robust. Sometimes such wines are lacking in scent.
Meaty	Same as fleshy, chewy, and beefy.
Noble	Wines with aristocratic traits: finesse, sophistication, breeding, balance.
Oaky	Wines with excessive amounts of oak flavors.
Off	A flawed or spoiled wine.
Off-taste	An unpleasant scent or taste.

Oxidized	Wines that have scents and tastes of vinegar and/or old dank sherry.
Ponderous	A wine that is too big and powerful. These are unbalanced "top-heavy" wines.
Pricked	Wines with noticeable amounts of acetic acid (vinegar).
Pruney	Uncomplimentary term. Prune flavor comes from wines that are made from overripe grapes. However, in wines such as Amarone where dried fruit flavors are common, the term is acceptable.
Refined	Polished and well-bred wines high in alcohol and loaded with rich flavorful extracts.
Robust	Rich, mouth-filling wines, masculine styled, high in alcohol, good acidity, and soft tannins. These are hearty, rich and very drinkable wines.
Rough	Wines with sharp, uneven qualities—high levels of acids, tannins, or alcoholic heat.
Round	Wines without the sharp edges of excessive acidity or high levels of scabrous tannins.
Scabrous	Term relating to rough aggressive tannins.
Savory	Flavorsome, supple, sapid, round wines are called savory.
Silky	Well-balanced, lush, soft, smooth, supple wines.
Stalky	Wines with the green, vegetal, and green twig scents.
Supple	Wines that are pleasing and easy to drink. No harsh acidity or rough tannins.
Tight-knitted	The elements in the wine are compacted and not easy to discern—bud like.
Twiggy	Same as stalky.

Ullage	The larger than normal empty space above the liquid in a bottle of wine. This is due to natural evaporation as wine ages or to a faulty cork. The later condition is more ominous. Wines with faulty corks are likely to be on their way to spoilage. Wines from the same case with different levels of ullage are likely to be due to a faulty cork
Vegetal	Wines that have vegetal tastes and smells– usually made from unripe grapes.
Woody	Wines with too much oaky flavor.

Wine and Your Health

The emphasis on health issues so prevalent in today's culture has spurred a renewed interest in wine. Wine is a remarkable health tonic that has been shown to prolong life and increase the quality of life. However, health benefits are derived only by the moderate consumption of wine; heavy drinkers have a considerably shorter live span. Moderate consumption is less than one-half bottles for men and one-fourth bottle for women. Maximum health benefits are achieved by daily consumption. The chart below lists some of the many health benefits of red wine.

Health Benefits of Red Wine
Wine decreases the incidence of many types of cancer including breast and prostrate.
Wine decreases the incidence of cardiovascular disease (heart attacks and strokes).
Wine decreases coronary spasm that can produce chest pain.
Wine increases HDL Cholesterol (good Cholesterol).
Wine decreases LDL Cholesterol (bad Cholesterol).
Wine decreases the incidence of non-insulin dependent diabetes.

Wine does not raise blood sugar and therefore can be used in the diabetic diet.
Wine does not raise blood sugar and therefore can be used in low carbohydrate diets such as Adkins, South Beach, and Zone.
Wine has antibacterial and antiviral qualities.
Wine aids in the digestion of food.
Wine relaxes broncospasm associated with asthma (provided that asthma was not caused by allergic reaction to some of the elements in the wine).
Wine has a calming effect.
Wine decreases the incidence of gall bladder disease.
Wine decreases the incidence of kidney stones.
Wine in moderation decreases the severity of osteoporosis.
Wine decreases the incidence of Alzheimer's disease and senile dementia.
Wine decreases the incidence of rheumatoid arthritis
Wine decreases the incidence of macular degeneration—a leading cause of blindness
Wine increases life expectancy.
Alcohol increases the incidence of breast cancer. Resveratrol a compound in red wine counters this effect. Red wine is the safest alcoholic beverage for women to drink.
Still wines (not carbonated) contain substances that delay the absorption of alcohol. This lessens the chance of becoming inebriated. A note of caution: carbonated beverages such as sparkling wines and drinks made with seltzer water increase the absorption of alcohol which increases the risk of becoming inebriated.

Serving Temperatures for Wines

Wines that are served too warm have high levels of aroma and flavor, but they are diffuse and not focused. For example, you might be able to say that the wine has berry flavors, but you will be unable to pick out the specifics: blackberries, raspberries, strawberries, etc. Wines that are served too cold have lower levels of flavors. The wine feels tight and unyielding. Wines served at the proper temperature will have all of its flavors in focus, you will be able to pick out the particulars: black currants, raspberries, strawberries, cherries, tobacco, leather etc. In general, serve lighter wines cooler than heavier wines, serve tannic wines warmer than less tannic wines, and serve sweet wines warmer than dry wines.

Red Wines	
Most red wines	60-65 degrees F
Beaujolais	55 degrees F
Highly tannic reds	65 degrees F
Lighter reds	55degrees F

White Wines	
Most white wines	55-60 degrees F
Full bodied whites (Chardonnay, Viognier, White Rhone)	55-65 degrees F
Light to medium bodied white wines (Riesling, Sauvignon Blanc)	50-55 degrees F
Dry Sherry	50 degrees F
Dessert Rieslings (Auslese, BA, TBA)	55 degrees F
Champagne	40-45 degrees F

Fortified Wines	
Sherry	55-60 degrees F
Oloroso/Amontillado Sherry	65 degrees F
Tawny Port	55-65 degrees F
Vintage Port	65 degrees F

Verdelho Madeira	50degrees F
Bual Madeira	55 degrees F
Malmsey Madeira	65 degrees

If you are a perfectionist, you can purchase a wine thermometer for bringing wine to the proper drinking temperature. There is also a handy device that will cool or warm a wine to the proper temperature that is sold by Sharper Image. However, for the usual assortment of table wines, the 20-20 rule is a simple method for obtaining a satisfactory drinking temperature.

The 20-20 rule: Place room temperature red wines in the refrigerator 20 minutes before you plan to serve them. Take fully chilled white wines out of the refrigerator 20 minutes before you expect to serve them. This treatment will be satisfactory for most wines.

ACKNOWLEDGMENTS

Fischer John
The Evaluation of Wine
Writers Club Press, 2001

Johnson, Hugh & Holliday, James
The Vintner's Art, How Great Wines Are Made
Simon & Schuster Inc., New York, 1992

Laube, James
California's Great Cabernets
Wine Spectator Press, San Francisco, California, 1989
California Wine
Wine Spectator Press, New York, 1995

Parker, Robert M.
Parker's Wine Buyer's Guide
Simon & Schuster Inc, New York, 1989
Burgundy

Parker, Robert M.
Bordeaux
Simon & Schuster Inc., New York, 1985

Parker, Robert M.
Wines of the Rhone Valley and Provence
Simon & Schuster Inc., New York, 1987

Peynaud, Emile
The Taste of Wine
The Wine Appreciation Guild Ltd, San Francisco, California, 1987
Knowing and Making Wine
Wiley-Interscience a division of John Wiley & Sons, Inc., 1984

Robinson, Jancis
Vines, Grapes, and Wines
Alfred A. Knopf, New York, 1986

Rosengarten, David & Joshua Wesson
Red Wine with Fish
Simon & Schuster

Shanken, Marvin R.— Editor and Publisher
Wine Spectator Magazine's Ultimate Guide To Buying Wine, 1995 Edition
M. Shanken Communications Inc, New York, 1994

Shanken, Marvin R. – Editor and Publisher
Eat Well, Drink Well, Live Longer
Wine Spectator, Dec 15th, 2001 issue

Scholten, Paul
Wine and Health
The International Wine and Food Society

Schoonmaker, Frank
The New Frank Schoonmaker Encyclopedia of Wine completely revised by Alexis Bespaloff
William Morrow & Company, Inc., New York,1988

Simon, Joanna
Discovering Wine
Simon & Schuster Inc.

Printed in the United States
133365LV00002B/75/A